A BETTER MAN

◆◆◆◆

A Better Man

◆◆◆◆

A (Mostly Serious) Letter to My Son

MICHAEL IAN BLACK

ALGONQUIN BOOKS
OF CHAPEL HILL
2020

Published by
ALGONQUIN BOOKS OF CHAPEL HILL
Post Office Box 2225
Chapel Hill, North Carolina 27515-2225

a division of
WORKMAN PUBLISHING
225 Varick Street
New York, New York 10014

Library of Congress Cataloging-in-Publication Data

Names: Black, Michael Ian, [date]– author.
Title: A better man : a (mostly serious) letter to my son / Michael Ian Black.
Description: First edition. | Chapel Hill, North Carolina : Algonquin Books
of Chapel Hill, [2020] | Summary: "Michael Ian Black takes a poignant
look at manhood, written in the form of a heartfelt letter to his teenage
son before he leaves for college. Black offers a radical plea for rethinking
masculinity and teaching young men to give and receive love"—
Provided by publisher.
Identifiers: LCCN 2019051609 | ISBN 9781616209117 (hardcover) |
ISBN 9781616209513 (e-book)
Subjects: LCSH: Men—Identity. | Masculinity. | Conduct of life. |
Fathers and sons.
Classification: LCC HQ1090 .B538 2020 | DDC 305.31—dc23
LC record available at https://lccn.loc.gov/2019051609

10 9 8 7 6 5 4 3 2 1
First Edition

For tomorrow's boys

◆◆◆◆

"[I]t was with a little surprise, and a little shame, that I realized my eldest son was only a summer away from leaving home for college, and I hadn't taught him, or the other kids, how to cook."
—CAL PETERNELL, *Twelve Recipes*

"Macho, macho man
I've got to be a macho man"
—VILLAGE PEOPLE

CONTENTS

A BETTER MAN

◆◆◆◆

The Wilds of Connecticut

WE MOVED TO our little Connecticut town when you were two. Mom was pregnant with Ruthie, and we'd outgrown our first home, a little Dutch Colonial in Peekskill, New York. We wanted a place with better schools, maybe a little more outdoor space. A friend had just moved here with his family, and he suggested we take a look. One bright autumn day as the holidays approached, we strapped you into your car seat and came to see for ourselves. The town seemed lovely and safe, the area schools all highly rated.

The thing that really got me, though, were the Christmas lights. Back in Peekskill, people decorated their homes like used car lots, gaudy red and green flashing lights wrapped in loose bunches around window frames and light posts. Inflatable Santas, plastic reindeer tipping drunkenly on roofs. I have always been a humbug when it comes to Christmas, and the rowdy Peekskill aesthetic only made me humbuggier. Here, in the demure Constitution State, it looked as if Martha Stewart had personally strung each home's holiday lights.

We bought a house and settled into it with our two-year-old son and new baby girl. We put some chairs on the front porch and watched the seasons change. I jokingly began calling our new town "the wilds of Connecticut" because, although we really do live in the woods, it felt like a Disney wilderness. The creatures, abundant though they may be, all seemed adorable: deer and foxes and wild turkeys and a lazy black bear the townsfolk nicknamed Bobbi. Sometimes though, late at night, we would hear an eerie music coming from the woods. A wild chorus of high-pitched keening. Coyotes after a kill. Mom and I would lie in bed and listen and, after a few minutes, it would stop.

One morning, several years after moving, I woke

you guys up for school. It was December, the sun late to rise. By this point in your school careers, the routine felt automatic, familiar to every parent. "Time to wake up." Mumbles. Breakfast cereal and orange juice. Shoes, jackets, backpacks. Lunches in lunchboxes. Peanut butter and jelly. Carrot sticks. An Oreo. Walk with you to the end of the driveway to wait for the bus, watch our breath in the cold morning air. Wave goodbye as the bus pulls away.

I came back into the house and sprawled on the living room couch. Mom was still in bed. I opened my laptop, did some work, glanced at Twitter, and there it was: gunshots at the elementary school next to ours. Sandy Hook.

The first reports didn't seem too bad, which sounds absurd even to say. One injury, a ricocheted bullet into the foot of a student. Police and ambulances arriving on the scene. I turned on the TV, flipped to the local news station. Nothing. Mom came down in her pajamas. I told her what I'd seen online, but the TV networks weren't covering it.

Maybe it was a false alarm? An Internet hoax?

A few minutes later, CNN broke into its morning programming: active shooter situation, teachers and children. Children. They may have given some initial, low estimate of the number of dead and wounded, I don't remember, but I do recall one of the reporters warning viewers that things were about to get "much, much worse."

Did they already know about Classroom 8, where fourteen first graders and two teachers were killed?

Did they know yet about Classroom 10, where four children and two teachers lay dead? (A fifth child would later be pronounced dead at the hospital.) One of the teachers, Anne Marie Murphy, was found trying to shield a child's body with her own.

A few miles away, your school went into lockdown. "Lockdown." When I was in school, that word didn't exist outside of prisons. School administrators activated the emergency phone system and sent out emails: "Your children are safe."

We waited. We watched TV. State troopers and SWAT teams and kids being led from the building, hands on the shoulders of the child in front of them.

Empty ambulances waiting for wounded that never came.

We got another email from your school explaining they weren't going to tell the kids what had happened because parents may wish to explain it in their own way. How do you explain mass murder to children whose only experience with death was a dead hamster laid to rest, with proper funeral rites, in the backyard? How do you explain to your kids that a young man could march into their school with a Bushmaster .223-caliber semiautomatic rifle and start firing at will? The email didn't say.

Mom and I watched TV off and on until the school buses brought you both home. We went out to the end of the driveway to meet you and walked, hand in hand, back to the house. "Was it really windy out today?" Ruthie asked.

"I don't think so," I said. "Why?"

"They said we couldn't have recess outside today because it was too windy."

When we got inside, we gathered you both together and told you. I don't even know what we said:

Something awful had happened. A bad man, but he was gone now. A lot of kids got hurt, but you didn't need to worry because you were both safe. Even as the words came out of my mouth, they felt like a lie. How could I promise your safety? I couldn't. My tongue felt slick, as if it were covered in gun oil.

When we finished, we asked if you understood. Yes, you both said. Did you have any questions? No. Were you okay? Yes, you were both okay. Could you go play now? Yes. You ran off separately, Ruthie to play with her American Girl dolls, you to finish the intricate wooden train track you were building in the playroom.

We had dinner. We put you to bed. We kept the TV off. Mom and I lay in bed and talked about keeping you home the next day, but decided against it. You would go to school tomorrow like always. We would place you back into the world and hope. That night, we listened to the woods and heard nothing.

When morning came, Mom and I got up together. "Time for school," breakfast, packed lunches: turkey sandwiches, raisins. Extra Oreos. We walked you to the bus and waved goodbye.

Parents know they can only do so much to protect their kids. We strap you into car seats, give you swim lessons. We offer advice, bundle you against the cold. But we can't do everything. Every parent knows this and accepts it. We do what we can and hope for the best. But this felt different. It felt like a tornado touching down, mindless and cruel. But also predictable. Infuriatingly predictable.

Everybody knew something like this would happen. Here, in America, it happens regularly. Mass shootings are as common as sunsets. Three shot, one dead at an apartment complex parking lot in Tulsa. Four dead at a Waffle House in Nashville. One sailor murdering two others before killing himself near a military hospital in Portsmouth, Virginia. Domestic violence. Suicide. Stories that barely get a mention on the local news before the sports report. People getting shot just isn't much of a story in America. We're used to it. This time, though, was different. This was children, twenty of them, and six adults.

The nation responded to Sandy Hook the way it always does when sensational acts of violence take place. People gathered. They held hands and lit candles and sang. News trucks rolled into town. Politicians laid out solemn offerings of "thoughts and prayers" like cold cuts at a wake. One by one, parents lowered their children into the ground. One after the other after the other. The president came. "We can't tolerate this anymore," he said. "These tragedies have to end."

He spoke beautifully about the need for change.

Nothing changed.

As I write these words in mid 2019, it's happened 2,135 more times. I'm only including mass shootings, defined as "events in which four or more people, excluding the shooter, were shot but not necessarily killed at the same general time and location." By the time you read this, that number will almost certainly be over 2,500.

No statistic recognizes that each death is a tornado, spinning countless lives into chaos. Six years after the shooting, one of the Sandy Hook fathers, who'd spent the intervening years researching brain disorders that can be related to violence, took his own life. Unexpectedly losing a loved one ends your world. That's what these bullets are, world enders.

Like a lot of people, I've been paying attention to the phenomenon of school shootings since two white teenage boys shot up their high school in Columbine, Colorado, in 1999. At the time, there wasn't even a term for these events. Headlines called it a "high school massacre," a "school attack," a "gun spree." When Columbine happened, we stupidly thought it was an aberration.

Then came all the others: schools in Georgia, New Mexico, Oklahoma, Michigan, Florida, Louisiana, California, New York . . . nearly every state, often multiple times. Then came Parkland, the deadliest high school shooting in American history. Seventeen high school students killed at Marjory Stoneman Douglas High School in Florida on Valentine's Day, 2018. Once again, we went through our national ablutions: the news crews, the thoughts and prayers, the resolutions to change. The failure to change.

You can go online and watch the interrogation of the Parkland shooter. It's ten hours long. The most striking thing about him is how young he looks. He's nineteen but looks younger. He sits in a plastic chair, his ankle shackled to a metal ring in the floor. He wears a hospital gown, his back exposed, his skinny frame visible when he moves. In the beginning of the interrogation, alone in the room, he shouts, "Kill me!" He bites at his arm.

Later, his brother comes in, a brother who apologizes for pushing the shooter away during their childhoods, blaming his own insecurities for the distance between them. At one point, he asks the interrogating officer if he can give his brother a hug. Yes. When he does, the shooter breaks down, sobbing.

"They're saying you're a monster," the brother says at one point.

"A monster?" the shooter responds, almost in disbelief.

If I hadn't known what he had just done, I would have had the same reaction. He doesn't look like a monster. To me, he just looks like some kid. Somebody's son. You can go through the list of mass shooters and you'll find the same thing in all of them: it's always somebody's son because it's always a boy. Girls aren't usually pulling the triggers in these massacres. It's boys.

I'm not going to pretend to understand gun violence, but I think I understand at least a couple components of it. The first is easy access to guns. You've heard me rail against the gun industry and its bloody mouthpiece, the NRA. I've called the NRA a terrorist organization because I believe that they not only know that easy access to guns will induce more slaughter, but, on some level, they want those killings to take place because gun sales skyrocket each time one happens. If we wanted to reduce shootings, all shootings, the first thing we would do is reduce access to guns.

The other component I think I understand, at least a little, is the way traditional masculinity can nudge a teetering psyche toward violence. Mass shootings are only the most sensational manifestation of our peculiar male dilemma: traditional manhood funnels the full range of male emotion into two channels, anger and withdrawal. Thankfully, most boys are resilient enough to resist these pressures and make positive contributions to the world. But some are not. Some will curl toward themselves like ingrown toenails. We've seen what those boys can do.

Traditional masculinity encourages strength, independence, fortitude. All good qualities. At the same time, though, it provides no useful outlets for our vulnerability. If we cannot allow ourselves vulnerability, how are we supposed to experience wonder, fear, tenderness? If we cannot turn to others for help, what do we do with bewilderment and frustration? How do we even express something as elemental as joy?

It's why the caricature of men is that we're simple creatures. George Carlin has a great joke: "Here's all you have to know about men and women: women are crazy, men are stupid. And the main reason women are crazy is that men are stupid."

Women aren't crazy and men aren't stupid, but the joke speaks to the limited ways we see each other and the frustrations that women, in particular, have with men. There's nothing wrong with our brains. Our brains are intact, fully functioning, nicely wrinkled. The problem is our emotional intelligence. And the reason our emotional intelligence is so low is that too many men only allow themselves those two basic modes of expression, anger and withdrawal.

For years, I was one of those guys. I cultivated an entire comedic persona based on withdrawal. If you ever want to see what that looks like, go watch me on one of those VH1 "I Love the . . ." shows in which talking heads reminisce about decades gone by. My segments are all totally deadpan, unsmiling, sarcastic. They were funny (if I do say so myself), but sarcasm is a form of withdrawal. I was good at it because by that point in my life, I had invested years learning how to act as if I didn't care about anything. What you see on TV is an exaggeration of the way I lived my life, but only a little. I had so much anger back then that I didn't know what to do with, so I clamped down. My release was jokes. They escaped like occasional steam puffs shaking the lid from a boiling pot.

The more successful I became doing that, the less satisfied I felt because I knew there was something fundamentally dishonest about it. That stone-faced person wasn't me anymore. I was recently married. I had a newborn son. Within a couple years, I would have a daughter. The person I saw onscreen, the one who never cracked a smile, didn't seem like he was ready to be a husband and a father. Maybe he wasn't ready. I began feeling a conflict between the person I found myself portraying on television and the man I was trying to become in real life. Maybe that shouldn't have mattered; after all, actors and comedians pretend. That's the job. But it mattered to me.

I wanted to be more open and honest in my life and in my work, which meant I had to change. Which meant I had to start asking myself some hard questions about who I was and what I valued. I had to pry apart the careful persona I'd constructed. I wanted to be a better husband and father. I wanted to be a better man.

For years, I thought there was something wrong with *me* (and don't get me wrong, there's plenty wrong with me), without considering the idea that some of the stuff screwing me up might be doing to the same to boys and men in general.

After Parkland, I began reconsidering. Why are boys committing these acts of violence? Why are boys falling behind girls in school? How do we teach young men to be respectful toward women? Why are men, and in particular white men, killing themselves in ever greater numbers? Is there really something "toxic" about masculinity? If so, what do we do about it? Is the role of men changing, and what does that mean for you?

You're eighteen and about to leave home for college. I wanted to give you something useful before you go. But what?

"Cash," you said, when I asked.

Fair enough, but I also wanted to offer something a little longer lasting. That's how I came to write this. Look, I'm not a sociologist, historian, psychologist, philosopher, or gender theorist. I have no qualifications to write this aside from one: I'm your dad.

I've spent the last year and a half doing a lot of reading and thinking about this topic. Now I'm trying put my thoughts down for you, and for parents like me who want to understand boys and men a little bit better. Take from it what you want. Discard what you don't. Some of the personal stories in here you've heard, some you've heard only in part. Some you've never heard at all. It's advice, a memoir, ideas, a primer. Or maybe I'm just having the conversation I wish my father could have had with me when I was starting out in the world. Maybe it's partially me talking to him now, man to man. Mostly, though, this is for you as you walk out the door. One father's love letter to his son.

ONE

◆◆◆◆

Some Guy

Now You're Home

Dear Elijah,

If you ever want to feel useless, I recommend attending the birth of your child. Mom and I had signed up for birthing classes together in anticipation of your arrival, but that preparation mostly involved learning how to count to ten over and over again in short breathy bursts. If you think that sounds like it would be a waste of time in the maelstrom of a delivery room, let me assure you, it is.

Mom's labor lasted almost a day. It was awful. At least it looked awful. Mom was in so much pain. I didn't know what to do. It's such a helpless feeling knowing that your partner is exhausted and in terrible pain and, in that moment, almost certainly hates you.

"Get it out!" Mom screamed at me. She was wrung out and desperate. I hovered nearby, stupidly counting to ten. "Stop counting!" Mom yelled. I stopped.

Finally, after twenty-two hours and a lot of drugs (for Mom, not me), there you were, flailing for the first time in the vast, unknowable air like Wile E. Coyote after he runs off the cliff.

As soon as you were born, the first thing the doctor did was announce to us your sex.

"It's a boy," she said.

In that first moment—after all the anticipation, all the guessing and name-picking and speculation—the fact of your boyness felt trivial, inconsequential. There you were, our child, our baby. What difference did your sex make? None, as far as I could tell. That's what I would have said if somebody had asked in the moment, but now I feel like that's not true.

"It's a boy," says the doctor, and everybody's brain makes a little mental click. What was just a baby the moment before is now a baby boy. Immediately, unconsciously, the endless possibilities for this new life narrow. The brain darts to "boy stuff": baseballs, toy trucks, dirt bikes, Nerf guns, electric guitars. "A boy," and without my even noticing it happen, my thoughts about you reordered, the way a new function reorders an algebraic equation.

Of course, this *shouldn't* be so. Of course, the horizons for any new life *should* remain boundless, regardless of sex. But society is not there yet, and pretending otherwise doesn't change that fact. I remain dubious of the new breed of parent attempting to raise "gender-neutral" kids. While I admire the spirit of the idea, I don't think it's possible and I don't know that it's even desirable. Like all people, kids crave a sense of self, an understanding of how they fit into the world. I think gender identity is an important part of this understanding of self. There's a big difference, though, between trying to impose traditional gender signifiers on a kid and letting the kid teach you who they are.

Any baby born with a penis is going to become aware pretty quickly that he's in this category called "boy." What he does with that boyness, though, should be up to him. As parents, I feel like our job is as much about listening and responding to our children as it is about steering them toward a desired outcome. A child will always tell you who they are—I don't mean just about gender, I mean about *everything*. You can either go with it or resist. In my experience as a dad, resistance is futile.

In the immediate moments after your birth, though, all those lessons were ahead of me.

There you were. And you were wonderful in the literal sense of the word. We looked at you and marveled at you and inspected you and the reality of you began to settle over us like the first flakes of snow in a blizzard. We'd known you'd be arriving soon, and here you were. Now we knew something about you. We knew what you were—not a puppy, not a chicken Parmesan—a baby human. A baby boy. But that was all we knew. Everything had changed and nothing had changed at all. The riddle of you remained.

"Do you want to cut the cord?" the doctor asked me, handing me a pair of lobster-claw scissors. I hadn't expected this, hadn't practiced for it. Cut the cord? In all those weeks of parenting classes, nobody said anything about performing *surgery*. It felt cruel. Your mom had held you tight for nine months, and now my first job as your father was to separate you from her? I didn't want to do it, nor did I want to say no because saying no would have, I thought, made the doctor and nurses question my manliness. I wasn't going to fail my very first task of fatherhood. So I grimaced and snipped through your umbilical cord, squishy like sausage casing.

The nurses swaddled you in a blanket and put one of those knitted blue caps onto your head, your very first clothing already telling the world something about the way it should think of you. We spent some time with you, holding you, touching your fingers and toes to make sure you were real, debating who you looked like. (You looked like a potato.) Mom held you to her chest. I took photos. They wheeled you to the nursery with all the other little blues and pinks.

Mom closed her eyes and I sat in a chair by the window trying out the word "dad" in my head.

Before I sat down to write this, I couldn't have told you the moment I felt I'd crossed, irrevocably, into manhood. Certainly not when I graduated high school. Nor when I turned eighteen. Definitely not when I dropped out of college to travel the country as a Teenage Mutant Ninja Turtle. Even when Mom and I got married, part of me still felt like a boy playing pretend. Here is the boy in his new suit standing at the altar. Here is the boy saying, "I do." Here is the boy wondering if everything will be okay. Here is the boy holding his son for the first time. Now, though, looking back, I know the moment. It was when I drove my family home from the hospital for the first time.

You were three days old. A nurse wheeled you and Mom out to the front entrance and I ran ahead to get our big white Jeep. I pulled up to the curb and helped Mom secure you into your car seat, a confusing tangle of straps and loops. Mom rode with you in the back-seat, me alone up front. Our house was less than two miles from that hospital but it felt like we had to cross a continent to get there. I've never been more terrified than the moment I turned out of the parking lot.

Let me just get them home, I thought.

Look right, look left, look right again. All clear. Turn

onto the road. Five miles below the speed limit. Drive. Left at the stop sign, chug up the hill to our street. A slow right at our road. Crawl onto the driveway. Shut off the car. Retrieve Mom's bag from the trunk. Ten steps to the front door. We cross inside. And there we are, home. The three of us: Mom, me, our baby boy whose name we haven't quite settled on.

I had the peculiar feeling of the world being different places: inside these walls and out. Outside, everything continued as it always had. Inside, everything was different. We showed you the house. "Here's the kitchen. Here's the dining room." We walked upstairs and showed you your room, the moon-and-stars mobile attached to your crib.

You spend nine months preparing for your baby's arrival. You might have a baby shower. You might take birthing classes. You might do a natural childbirth or you might get drugs (tell your partner to get the drugs). Everything is so focused on the baby's arrival, just like when you get married and everything is focused on the wedding day. But then the event arrives and the rest of your life begins. When Mom's contractions started, we left the house as one thing: a couple. We came back as another: parents. After we'd given you the house tour, I remember Mom and me turning to each other and one of us saying, "Now what?"

The answer to that question revealed itself over time. There was the immediate business of keeping you alive. Learning how to hold you so your head didn't flop over like an overgrown sunflower. Learning how to keep you clean and warm. Learning how to manage the resentment and rage that comes from lack of sleep. Mostly, though, learning how to love you.

It would be easy to tell you how over the moon I was when you came into our lives, but that's not true. I didn't fall in love with you, or your sister, at first sight. Maybe I had fallen for the myth that the mere sight of one's offspring sets to swooning the new parent's heart. That didn't happen for me. My friend Rob has three children, two girls and his youngest, a boy. When his son was born, he joked with me that he worried how weird it would feel to have another male among the women with whom he lived. "So now there's going to be some guy living in my house?" he said.

That's a little bit how it felt. Suddenly there was some guy living in the extra bedroom. Some guy demanding all of our attention. Some guy who loved my wife but didn't seem that crazy about me.

Over time, I figured, we would come to some accommodations as housemates. And we did. Or, rather, I came to some accommodations as to you. I woke when you woke. Ate when you allowed me. Entertained you and drove you around to your various appointments. Picked out your wardrobe. I did all the parenting stuff and, in doing so, fell in love with my baby boy.

It's funny; without even meaning to, I began thinking of you as my baby *boy*. How—or whether—that affected the way I parented you, I can't say. I didn't dress you exclusively in blue or make you sleep with a baseball mitt or anything hokey like that. I bought you all kinds of toys: old-fashioned (non-choking-hazard) wooden blocks and soft dolls and bright books with thick cardboard pages. I read to you and sang to you and, when you fussed, I sh-sh-shushed you on my shoulder, bouncing from foot to foot, rubbing your back in rhythmic circles.

I don't remember the first time you called me "dada," but I remember your wide gummy smile when I swung you around in my arms and your chubby legs and your wispy hair. I remember you toddling on unsteady feet. I remember wondering what I'd been so worried about when just the thought of you put a wobble in my own step. Why had I been so unsure about my ability to be your dad? Maybe it had been losing my own father at such a young age and my own conflicted emotions about him when he'd been alive.

TWO

Rosary

Tell Your Kids You Love Them

ONE OF MY favorite photos of my dad—your grandpa—
is also one of the last he ever took. He's thirty-nine. In
the photo, Dad wears a slight, embarrassed smile below
the goofy teddy bear baseball cap his wife Beth had
given him to cover the new scar that stretches across
his skull. He'd undergone emergency brain surgery
a couple months before, after the police found him
slumped over in his car, unconscious. An assault, they
thought. Maybe a mugging gone bad. They didn't know.
My mom told us about it the following morning. He
was going to be okay, she said, and I remember thinking something like, "Of course he's going to be okay."

I'd never considered that my father could be hurt, let alone die.

A few days later, your uncle Eric and I went to see him at the hospital. I remember him in bed, head shaved and bandaged, sleepy and frail, his body covered in a loose gown. I felt awkward and unsure and scared. His fragility frightened me more than anything else. He'd never been a big guy, but every father is a giant to his son, although less so when his son overtakes him in height, as you, annoyingly, have done to me. We stayed with him for an hour or so that day, but he didn't talk much, and when we left him, I felt relieved.

When Dad came home, he was weak and unsure on his feet. That Christmas, Beth gave him teddy bears. Lots of teddy bears, big and small. One of the bears was sewn to the brim of a baseball cap, the dumb hat in the photo. A few months later, he would be back in the hospital, where he died from a blood clot.

I remember that tight smile of his. It was his all-purpose smile. It could mean joy, sorrow, frustration, bafflement, or some combination of those. It's a smile unwilling to commit to emotion. Every now and again, I catch myself making that same smile and I get a tingle of déjà vu. It's funny—I look more like my mom. I have her coloring and some of her facial features. But I have never felt possessed by her in the same way I do when I discover my dead father's expression on my face.

One of the things that haunts me still is the ambivalence I felt about him when he was alive. My parents' divorce had been bitter, interminable. My mother's grievances with my father spilled into our daily conversations at home and, over the years, they poisoned my feelings toward him. Was he really, as she maintained, a sexist? Was he really not upholding his obligations to her, and to us? Did he really not love our younger sister, Susan, who has Down syndrome? I looked for proof of his failings and found it. Once, he bought me a baseball mitt for my birthday, a good gift until I realized he'd bought a right-handed glove. Didn't he know I am left-handed? Didn't he care? A simple mistake, but I filed it away as evidence against him.

I ignored the evidence in his favor. The trip to Indian Guides camp. The visits to the boardwalk on the

Jersey Shore to play Skee-Ball. The time he helped us carve our names out of wood blocks. The weekends we spent with his sister and her girls.

I have another photo of him. It might be the only one with the two of us together. I'm young, maybe five or six, which means he would have been in his early thirties. We're at the Guinness World Records Museum in New York City, posing in front of a giant (perhaps world record–holding) house of cards. I've got my hands shoved into the pockets of my puffy winter coat. My dad towers over me, his hand resting on my shoulder, that same smile on his face. I don't remember that trip, but I feel as though I remember the weight of his hand, the protection and love it held.

When my mom and dad first split up, Mom was already involved with her new girlfriend, the woman I call Elaine. As Mom and Dad's divorce proceedings got underway, a social worker took me into a room by myself to ask which parent I wanted to live with. How do you ask a five-year-old to choose between his parents? I started crying, and I remember the shame that accompanied those tears. I used to cry a lot, about everything. A disappointment. A sharp word. Tears from restlessness and frustration and rage. Mom used to say I was "sensitive." I fucking hated that word. Hated my own emotions because I knew, even at five years old, they made me feel weak. The social worker put me on her lap to comfort me. Who was she, this stranger, asking intrusive questions? Who was she to indulge in this forced intimacy? "Don't touch me!" I wanted to scream, but didn't. Instead, I made myself stop crying. It's the first time I remember consciously shutting down my emotions.

The divorce dragged on for years. Eventually, and over the objections of my father, Mom won custody of Susan, Eric, and me, with regular weekend visits to Dad. Throughout the divorce and for the rest of my childhood, we lived with Mom and Elaine in a suffocating townhouse in New Jersey. I hated living there.

Elaine had so much rage, a consuming heat that, day to day, threatened to burn our family down to nothing. We all suffered the heat of her temper, but she reserved the worst of it for her only child, a boy about my age I'll call Gary, whom she and her ex-husband had adopted as a baby. Gary was heavy and ungainly and sweet, at least until Elaine stamped the sweetness out of him. "Stupid," she called him. "Lazy." "An idiot." Words ripped out of the abuser's playbook. He was a loser, she said, and would never amount to anything. He could do nothing to please her. Eventually he stopped trying.

None of us stood up for him. It felt too dangerous.

Elaine's fire eventually spread to my mom, whose moods became brittle and fractured. Sometimes she would take her frustrations out on us kids, but more often she and Elaine directed their anger at each other. Their fights might last a few hours or a few weeks. During these times we boys would hide up in our bedroom or downstairs in the basement, speckled brown carpeting and thin wood paneling over Sheetrock. The only one who escaped the abuse was Susan, but her disability created its own tensions around money and social services and her endless medical needs.

I never told Dad about life at home. I don't think Eric did, either. We never asked to move in with him and Beth because I think we both suspected they wouldn't have wanted us to. Yes, he fought for custody of us, but I don't know if he really wanted us to live with him or if he was just putting up a fight as revenge toward Mom and the wounded pride I imagine he felt at the way she'd left him.

In the seven years between the time my parents split up and Dad's death, he never bought us beds. We slept in sleeping bags on the living room floor. We didn't mind, particularly, because we were kids, but the message felt unmistakable: "You are welcome here, but only for the weekend." Even after they bought the big house out in Plainsboro—the house had a sewing room for Beth but no bedroom for his kids.

Sometimes I wonder what your relationship with him would have been like. I think you would have liked each other, although I doubt you would have been close. I don't think he knew how to get close to people. He was too shy, too withdrawn, lived too much in his own head. He'd studied engineering and had an engineer's mind. He liked mechanical things, electronic things. He bought a computer from Radio Shack called the TRS-80. It was the first computer I'd ever seen, a bulky silver vision of the future that seemed to come straight out of his favorite show, *Star Trek*. The machine fascinated my dad, the same way computers and videogames fascinate you. Dad used to spend hours huddled at his desk just off the second-floor landing, seemingly preferring the company of his computer to that of his kids, even though we only saw him every other weekend. One of the reasons I say "I love you" to you and your sister every day is because my father never could bring himself to say the words to the three of us.

It hurts me to admit to you that he wasn't a very good dad. I am convinced he loved his kids, but didn't know what to do with that love. Maybe he worried that he didn't have enough and so he kept it in reserve, the way he kept emergency supplies in the trunk of his car. I know I loved him. I just didn't know how to break through and I was afraid to try. If I had to guess, I'd guess that he was afraid to try, too.

All these years later, I still wish I could hear my dad tell me he loved me. He never did. When I was younger, I used to think about what that cost me. Now, as a parent, I think about what it must have cost him. Imagine being unable to say the only three words that matter to your kids. When I tell you "I love you" as you head out the door in the morning, or I kiss your head good night, or after rolling my eyes at one of your gleefully horrible puns, I'm reminding you that, no matter what happens out there in the wider world, here you are valued and accepted. I'm trying to press it into your heart so that when circumstances turn against you, you will feel it imprinted there as a reminder, a rosary.

My father, Robert Michael Schwartz, was the first man I ever knew, and when he died he was the first person I ever knew who died. After you turned thirteen, I felt as though I'd reached a milestone because, no matter what happened from that point forward, at least you'd had me one year longer than I'd had my own dad. Without even knowing I'd been carrying it, I felt myself relieved of a burden. I felt the same way when your sister turned thirteen a couple years later. Although my relief was genuine, some part of me also felt as if I'd committed a small transgression by outliving my own father. Now I am older than he ever was by a decade and that feeling of transgression has been replaced by something else, some sense that I am walking with him, and for him.

A child doesn't recover from losing a parent. It ends your world, yet the world doesn't end. It's the strangest sensation to lose somebody you love, a pain inevitably compounded by the realization that not everybody shares your grief, that somehow life continues, largely indifferent to your loss.

The poet Eileen Myles wrote a memoir about their dog, Rosie, a dog that Myles said represented the longest adult relationship of their life. Early in the book, *Afterglow*, a vet puts the long-suffering Rosie to sleep. Afterward, Eileen sits with her, flowers decorating the dog's neck: "The world was outside the door. It was Saturday morning. . . . The world out there now on the other side of the wall. In here, just us."

That's just how I felt.

Even before Dad died, I sensed part of myself separating from the world. I suspect every person eventually feels themselves becoming untethered from the world and all the people in it at some point in their lives. Maybe that's what adolescence is, the discovery that everything seems one way, but we feel ourselves to be another. Perhaps maturation, then, is just the slow process of reattaching ourselves to the world and holding out a hand for those still out there in space, alone.

I think my own sense of isolation and detachment happened earlier than most, and I think it took me longer than most to recover my footing. Some of that had to do with my particular living circumstances, and part of it, I think, had to do with my own fuzzy notions of what it meant to be a man. Although I knew that I would one day become a man myself, the boundary between my boyhood self and the men I observed appeared to me impermeable. There was boyhood and there was manhood, and no obvious way to bridge the two.

Mom and Elaine didn't help. They considered themselves avid feminists, but their version of feminism took on a particularly acrid odor. They regularly denigrated men in front of the three boys living in their care. Men were arrogant and condescending and unreliable. They were "male chauvinist pigs," always less capable than the women beside them. Men would betray you. A movie came out called *9 to 5*, which was a feminist revenge

comedy about three underappreciated female employ-
ees who kidnap their sexist boss and run the business
in his stead, thereby proving that women can do the job
of a man better than he can. Mom and Elaine saw the
movie, and then took us boys to see it. The movie was
hilarious, its message unmistakable: men sucked.

It was a message I took with me into my teenage
years and early adulthood. I favored the company of
women to men. I had male friends, but my relationships with females always felt more intimate, which was
probably the reason I had girlfriends before so many of
my male peers, and probably why those relationships
lasted longer than typical first romances.

I also suspected the message was incomplete. Yes,
men sometimes suck. Yes, we could be all the things we
stood accused of being, and worse. We could be dangerous, and especially dangerous to women. But men,
I thought, were more than that, just as those women in
the movie were more than what their boss saw.

I worried that I carried some of that male sucki-
ness with me, worried that there was something wrong
with me simply for being a boy. But I liked being a boy.

And I wanted, one day, to be a man. To do that, I had to understand them. After my dad died, I didn't know how I ever would.

To my kid eyes, men seemed as if they possessed some secret magic. They seemed confident. They knew "things" about "things." They understood women and cars and rock 'n' roll. They could fix stuff. Men could conjure up seemingly unknowable facts from the air the way my uncle Larry would pull quarters from my ear. Men, I thought, understood the whole of the world. How did they learn so many things when, from my experience, they did so little actual communicating? The men I saw around me barely spoke at all; I thought their grunts and smirks and nods were a language just beyond the range of my hearing. One day, I figured, my father would pass these fraternal secrets to me, an intriguing alchemical mixture of aftershave, carburetor fluid, and tits.

He never did.

Just as I wonder what your relationship with him would be like, I wonder how he would have felt about today's world. Maybe he would have grown stodgy and bitter as he got older, the way so many white men of his generation have turned against the culture. Or maybe he'd already absorbed the shock of change in his younger years, and would have accommodated a new and potentially confusing way of life. I can tell you that even I find myself confused much of the time. When something as previously reliable as pronouns becomes a source of cultural contention, I can understand how somebody might feel bewildered.

My dad was a conformist right down to the marrow of his bones. I don't say that as a put-down. He grew up the son of a cop. Rules mattered, and the rules worked for my dad. There doesn't seem to be much sense in breaking the rules when they are to your benefit. Back then, the rules worked for most white men. I don't think he thought too much about problems beyond the ken of his own surroundings. That's not to say he was indifferent to the sufferings of others, but I don't recall him ever speaking to us about social or political issues.

What was it like for him when my mom left him for a woman? It would have been such an unexpected turn of events for a man who'd played by the rules his whole life to be confronted with a woman openly defying them for the first time in hers. To his credit, he never spoke ill of her in front of us kids, but I got the sense that he felt doubly betrayed by her adultery and its nature. Maybe that experience would have made him less receptive to the cultural changes we're experiencing now, or maybe it would have helped him better appreciate human complexity. I don't know. He was still a young man when he died, still knocking the tent poles of his own life into place.

I know that sense of dislocation. It would be hard for anybody living today not to. To say that we live in "an accelerating culture" has become a cliché; it feels more apt to say that speed *is* the culture. Most days I just want to keep up, but I don't want to be so anxious to keep pace that I end up losing what's worth preserving from the past. Sometimes it's not easy to distinguish between the things that have value and the things that don't.

I'm hoping you and your sister can help me. Your generation is going to have a lot to teach mine. The ideas I'm giving to you now are the best I can do *now*.

I hope you'll tell me where you think I've fallen short. I hope you'll remind me to stay open and available and receptive to new ideas. Maybe the last job of parenting is surrendering the lead and letting our kids guide us forward. We're going to need the help.

Does manhood mean something different today than it did ten years ago? One hundred years ago? Was it different for my dad than it is for me? Will it be still different for you? Or is manhood as steadfast as the moon, and it's only our perception of it that changes when the light shines from a different direction?

What does it mean to be a man?

THREE

◆◆◆◆

Skate or Die

You're Not Toxic

THERE USED TO be this T-shirt that had a graphic of a penitent-looking little boy with his hands folded in front of him. The caption read, "I know I'm somebody 'cause God don't make no junk." As a kid, I used to think about that slogan in terms of my sister. And as the child of a lesbian, I also used to think about it in terms of my mom and the fight for gay acceptance. (Forget actual gay *rights*: when I was a kid, we just wanted to keep our house from getting egged.) Now, though, I also relate it to the struggles of boys. If traditional masculinity is no longer working, I want to make clear it's not the fault of our biology. God don't make no junk, but people certainly do.

It's why I don't like the phrase "toxic masculinity." To me, the term implies that there's something inherently wrong with men, some poison baked into our Y chromosomes. Bullshit. You're not toxic, although I admit, you don't always smell so great after track practice.

I worry that the term "toxic masculinity" is a little like the phrase "New Jersey native." Both are impossible to hear without feeling a little defensive. I don't want you to feel that way about being a guy. Yes, be aware of certain bilious—and worse—behaviors men sometimes display. Yes, be sensitive to women's concerns for their safety and well-being. Yes, do the steady work of self-improvement. But I worry that continuously describing male expression as toxic has the cumulative effect of denying the goodness in men. Although men bear responsibility for so much of what's wrong in the world, we also provide some share of what's right. We work hard and provide for others. We are helpers and friends and nurturers. We sacrifice. We inspire.

Most of us have a hard enough time talking about our masculinity without also being subject to an immediate pejorative affixed to our sex. I worry that too many guys will reject the topic out of hand if the only time they hear the word is when it's linked to the worst impulses of our kind. I grew up feeling defensive about my gender after hearing my mom and Elaine belittling men. I don't want the same for you.

(You may not appreciate the irony of my concern about men feeling belittled for their gender, but women will. It's what men have been doing to them forever.)

Why has traditional masculinity found itself in the crosshairs?

When you kids were little, we used to wrestle a lot. You and Ruthie would try to pull me off the couch or the chair or some other stationary object from which I did not wish to be removed. Because you two were little and I was all-powerful, you rarely got very far in these efforts. That essentially describes every power structure humans have ever lived with. Somebody's on top of the heap and somebody else tries to knock them down. Might has always made right. Until very recent human history, the people with the most might have almost always been men for the simple reason that men, on average, are physically stronger than women.

It's embarrassing that something so stupid should be so fundamental to the way we learned to organize ourselves as humans, but it's the truth.

Proto-government systems were basically just the strongest dude of the bunch ordering everybody else around under threat of getting their teeth knocked out. Nearly all the governments that came after, whatever form they took, were based on this same premise. Do what the guy in charge says or get your head impaled on a spike, your limbs ripped apart by horses, or your innards pulled from your stomach. Powerful men have always figured out creative ways to impose their will on the unwilling.

Over the centuries, the idea of what constituted a "powerful man" evolved. Kings weren't necessarily the physically strongest people. Their power largely derived from their wealth—maybe accrued through inheritance or battle or a perceived one-on-one connection with God—which bought them the loyalty of the armed men at their disposal. The duties of these men mostly involved accumulating more wealth for their king in exchange for securing their own futures. Yes, women sometimes ruled in monarchic dynasties, but they were the exception. Their advisers were almost always men, the armies who defended their rule were comprised of men, the clerics who legitimized their rule through religion were, by and large, also men. In nearly every civilization across time, those who held power were of one sex.

To understand the history of men in our country, you have to understand the special role that white men have played in it. Our system of power is rooted in, and is still largely based on, white male dominance. This persistent "might" has led to feelings of supremacy. If you don't like that loaded term, you can just think of it as the status quo.

Acknowledging that fact is different from labeling all white Americans as "racist" in the sense of believing in, and advocating for, white supremacy. For most white Americans, I don't think that's the case. But—and this is a big "but"—even though most of us would never describe ourselves as racist, all Americans are born into a system built *upon* racism. It is as impossible to separate ourselves from that system as it is to separate the design of our bodies from our DNA. It's who we are. Our nation was built on the backs of black slaves. The institution of slavery ended over 150 years ago, but its effects remain with us in powerful and palpable ways that continue to inform every aspect of our American lives.

I'm telling you that because so much of the current American anxiety over "toxic masculinity" in the culture starts with the role of *white* men. The reason this conversation is happening now is because, for the first time, the traditional power structure is under threat. Here in America, that power structure has always been as male and white as George Washington's bare ass.

Why is our white male power structure under threat? The white part is easy to explain. As a percentage of the population, there are fewer white people than before and our numbers are decreasing. Fewer white people means, literally, less white power.

These demographic shifts are why some (white-skinned) people are working so hard to prevent (black- and brown-skinned) immigration, to disenfranchise so many (black- and brown-skinned) voters, and to concentrate the votes of as many (black- and brown-skinned) citizens as they can into grotesquely gerrymandered districts. New demographics may be destiny, but the status quo is doing everything it can to forestall the inevitable.

As for why the *male* part of the power structure is now under threat, you have to go back several steps. I could pick any number of places to start, but I'm going to begin on July 19, 1848 in Seneca Falls, New York. There, a thirty-three-year-old abolitionist delivered a talk entitled "Declaration of Sentiments" to a crowd of about 300 women at the event she organized, the first Women's Rights Convention. She wrote her speech as a counterargument to the Declaration of Independence, beginning:

> When, in the course of human events, it becomes necessary for one portion of the family of man to assume among the people of the earth a position different from that which they have

hitherto occupied, but one to which the laws of nature and of nature's God entitle them, a decent respect to the opinions of mankind requires that they should declare the causes that impel them to such a course.

The language is genteel, but make no mistake: Elizabeth Cady Stanton is throwing fists. Women, she's saying, are sick of occupying a secondary place "in the family of man" when the "laws of nature" entitle them to equality. They are therefore "impelled" to chart a new course. The petticoats are coming off.

She then turns the original Declaration's most famous phrase against itself:

We hold these truths to be self-evident: that all men and women are created equal; that they are endowed by their Creator with certain inalienable rights; that among these are life, liberty, and the pursuit of happiness; that to secure these rights governments are instituted, deriving their just powers from the consent of the governed.

Adding "and women" to the famous line about certain truths being self-evident creates a radical new understanding of the Declaration of Independence because it makes readily apparent that the government of the United States, in declaring its separation from England, has treated a majority of its people in the same injurious way that England had treated its colonists. A few million enslaved people could have told you the same thing.

Stanton and other white women were beginning to see the parallels between slavery and their own second-class citizenry. She asked an obvious question: how could a nation founded on the notion of equality hold women in subservience to men?

(By the way, you can't separate Elizabeth Cady Stanton's advocating for women from the question of race in America. Stanton's work on women's rights grew out of her work with the abolitionist movement. She and her husband, Henry Stanton, were prominent abolitionists. In fact, they were so devoted to the cause that they used their honeymoon to attend an antislavery conference in London, which doesn't sound like the most romantic way to start a marriage, but who am I to judge?)

So you had this new "women's rights" thing going on at the same time that America was undergoing another, more fundamental change. According to sociologist and writer Michael Kimmel in his eye-opening book, *Manhood in America: A Cultural History*, for much of our early history, men and women both provided for the family, sharing in the labor of family farms and small, family-run places of business. Then, the Industrial Revolution upended everything.

The small local family farms and businesses that had provided goods and services to their communities couldn't compete with cheaper, machine-made wares. Work began moving from rural areas to factories in cities. Families abandoned their old ways for a new, urban life in which men assumed responsibility for earning money while women took on ever more responsibility in the home. This created a starker delineation between the work of men and the work of women. What emerged is the relatively modern idea that men are solely responsible for providing for the family, the so-called "breadwinners."

Millions of men became "wage slaves," those whose survival depended on the industrialists to whom they rented their labor. Even the abolitionist Frederick Douglass, who freed himself from slavery, came to compare the average working man's salaried existence as not much better than the one he had left behind, saying that the experience of working on salary "demonstrates that there may be a slavery of wages only a little less galling and crushing in its effects than chattel slavery, and that this slavery of wages must go down with the other."

That's a hell of a thing for Douglass to say: the jobs required for men to survive in this new age were only "a little less galling and crushing" than slavery. Yet these jobs, as physically demanding, repetitive, and dangerous as they might have been, were still a man's best option for gainful employment. Better awful work than no work at all. The men who got these new jobs, white men, fought to keep them restricted from non-whites, who they feared would drive down already low wages. They did the same with women who wished to work beside them.

Women have always worked, of course, but their access to most kinds of modern employment was limited. That began to change in the first half of the twentieth century, when two world wars cracked the factory doors open for women. With so many men fighting overseas, women were needed to run the nation's industrial floors, disproving the widespread belief that they were not capable of doing the physically arduous work of men.

These new opportunities, coupled with women winning the right to vote in 1920, began a new phase in the fight for women's equality. That new phase fully emerged in the 1960s as a massive movement. This "second wave feminism" focused on a broad range of issues, including reproductive freedom, workplace rights, and pervasive sexism. It was during this time that my mom found herself open to the possibility of falling in love with the woman down the street.

Mom and Elaine thought of themselves as fervent feminists, but I'm not sure how much work they actually did for the movement. In my household, I understood feminism as mostly being about getting *Ms.* magazine in the mail every month, listening to my mom and Elaine talk about what a genius Lily Tomlin was, and sitting in silence at dinner as they unloaded about what some asshole man did at work that day.

Though obviously incomplete, women's progress over the last sixty years has been extraordinary. Women are now in a far better position to control their own lives, including their sexual and reproductive choices. With greater access to all kinds of work, they are better able to provide for themselves and others. No longer tied to a man's ability to earn money, they are better able to be independent, to enter relationships as equals, and to exit unhappy relationships without as much fear of financial or social ruin.

The white men in this country who once dominated the paid labor force are now competing on a more level playing field with women, minorities, and workers from around the globe. Even the nature of work has undergone a transformation, moving from the physical to the cerebral. Education, creativity, and analytic thinking have replaced brawn as the chief qualifications for employment.

The result is that now we've got a bunch of dudes— and in particular white dudes—trying to figure out who they are because the things that used to define us as distinct from women no longer do. Men's sense of identity, community, and purpose has blurred.

When you combine the rise of women, technological disruption, and the demographic inevitability that white people will soon become a majority minority in America, the question about why we are having this conversation about "toxic masculinity" now answers itself: This is the first time this conversation *could* happen. It is the first time that white male dominance has been under serious threat.

What happens when men are no longer the only ones out there doing "man stuff"? How do men react? I think there are two possible answers, and we're seeing both of them play out in real time.

The first option is retreat. This is the Mar-a-Lago approach, in which white guys huddle behind castle walls yelling at Fox News. It's a way for white men to insulate themselves against their own fading relevance, a way to preserve a time that was. It may also mean trying to hang on to the rigid masculinity of our fathers and grandfathers, a masculinity that seeks, above all else, control.

The second option is to adapt. When I was a kid, there was this videogame I used to like where you were in a skateboard park and had to perform increasingly difficult tricks to gain points. If you failed to land your tricks or didn't travel far enough, a swarm of hornets would attack you and a booming voice would call out, *"Skate . . . or die!"* That's kind of where I feel like guys are right now. Skate or die.

You're entering adulthood at an incredible time for men. You have the opportunity to be part of a conversation about the new shape of manhood. If you want it to, your generation of men can become pioneers, reinventing masculinity the same way women continue to adapt femininity. We men have an advantage that they didn't, though, which is that women have already shown us what's possible. For the last hundred years, women have led the way. Now it's time for us to confront a stifling view of traditional masculinity and figure out a new, more productive way to exist as men. There has to be a way to retool masculinity for an age that demands something more from men. There has to be a model that prizes empathy and cooperation as much as strength and independence.

Empathy is so important because it's the door we have to walk through to find compassion, understanding, altruism. Children of both sexes start displaying empathy around the age of two. It just bubbles out of them like snot. Why push against who we already are? We should work on empathy with our sons at least as much as we work on their batting stances. Empathy doesn't make a man weak; it gives him a compass to follow when he needs to be strong.

Yes, men are flawed. Because people are flawed. We're also scared. Not just because of the external world, but because of our internal one. The great unacknowledged truth about men is that the traditional masculinity meant to project strength often masks terror. Men feel isolated, confused and conflicted about our natures. Many feel that the very qualities that used to define men—strength, aggression, and independence—are no longer wanted or needed; many others never felt strong or aggressive or independent to begin with. We don't know how to be, and we're terrified.

But to even admit our terror is to be reduced, because we don't have a model of masculinity that allows for fear or grief or tenderness or the day-to-day sadness that sometimes overtakes us all. Too many of us are trapped in the same suffocating, outdated model of masculinity, where manhood is measured in strength, where there is no way to be vulnerable without being emasculated, where manliness is about having power over others. We don't even have the language to talk about how we feel about being trapped, because the language that exists to discuss the full range of human emotions is still viewed as "feminine," and above all else, traditional masculinity rejects femininity. We're trapped and we're terrified and it's killing us. That's why we have to change.

I think it's important to acknowledge that straight dudes, and especially straight *white* dudes like you and me, have had it easier than every other group in America and continue to do so. We can point that out and still recognize that straight white dudes are suffering, too, and that our problems relate to the same problems other groups face. But they are also distinct in a lot of ways, resulting from our historic position of privilege in America.

This privilege sometimes expresses itself in the most grotesque ways. I don't think it's a coincidence that school shooters are nearly always male, their ethnicity almost always white. Why? I think it's because school shootings are the ultimate manifestation of white male privilege. These guys aren't content to merely destroy themselves; they want to destroy the entire world. That thought process, and the level of self-importance required to see one of these massacres through, requires astonishing arrogance. Here in America, that arrogance is most commonly associated with one demographic: the straight white male.

It would be easy to lay the entirety of our nation's problems at the feet of its straight white men. That's not my intention. Instead, I'm trying to tell you why I believe it's way more complicated than that. Not because, historically, we haven't caused most of these problems, but because we, too, are now suffering from many of these same problems, and we, too, need a way out. The relentless American marketing campaign of the Real Man has fucked a lot of us up.

The problems with our men can't be viewed in isolation from other massive problems we have as a nation. A lot of it boils down to this: despite all of its self-congratulatory, flag-waving exuberance, America is not a meritocracy. Yes, anybody *can* make it here, but it doesn't mean they will. One of the most determinate factors in where you go in America is the zip code in which you were born. According to the Economic Policy Institute, among wealthy nations, the United States is close to the bottom in socioeconomic mobility. You've got a better shot at living out the American dream in Japan than you do in America. We're starting to see the American dream run right through our fingers. And not just the dream, but much of what we already have: home ownership levels are declining; even if it's available, affordable health insurance is threatened; job security is practically nonexistent. So when you hear about American voters experiencing "economic anxiety," there's a good reason for that. They are. And if you think "economic anxiety" is also sometimes used by politicians as racist code to cast the blame for these large-scale economic changes on immigrants and those born into less fortunate circumstances than the vaunted (white) "middle class," congratulations, you speak American.

Men, all men, fear their entire way of being is threatened because it *is* being threatened. Men do not know whom to blame, so we often cast a suspicious eye on groups who seem to be making progress as we seem to falter. A good friend of mine, a guy you know, said he supports more women moving into his male-dominated profession but worries: "I've worked for women, and I've had women work for me and I've never had a problem with it," he told me. But now he thinks maybe it's going too far. "It might cost me a job," he said.

"You're right," I told him.

Progress brings change. Change brings tumult. America is in the midst of a deep, fretful conversation about nearly every aspect of our national character. It's a conversation America has had in fits and starts since its founding. We've fought about who we are from the moment we became a nation. Are we wild pioneers or pious parishioners? Cowboys or corporatists? The roles of women, African Americans, immigrants, gays and lesbians, rich and poor have all been analyzed. Now our attention is turning to America's men. Men are bedrock, foundational. But even foundations crack, and now this one has, too.

For those who have suffered under that system for centuries, it's no doubt tempting to say, "Welcome to the club. Deal with it." And I don't blame anybody who says that, but if I am going to have empathy and compassion for those who have historically suffered, I also need to have empathy and compassion for those who are feeling that pain for the first time. That might mean you. If we can figure out a way to deal with these issues together, we'll all be better off. Besides, you're my kid and I love you—even if you are a straight white male.

♦♦♦♦

FOUR

A Useful Engine

You're a Real Man

I REMEMBER THE first time somebody told me I was being a boy wrong. I was very young, three or four years old. Mom and Dad were still together. We'd been invited to a neighbor's house for dinner, a rare event, and we must have shown up late because the house was already crowded when we arrived.

As we walked in, the family's giant black Labrador retriever scrambled over to greet us in the traditional manner of Labrador retrievers, which involves a lot of physical contact and an excess of sloppy dog kisses. Being three or four years old, I was unfamiliar with this custom. So when the dog jumped up on me, its enormous paws clamping on my shoulders, its wet and monstrous face in mine, I naturally thought it was trying to kill me. I screamed, terrified: "Get it off!"

The dog reacted in the same manner that our own Lab, Ole, reacts to my commands today—it ignored me. Worse, the adults expressed no urgency about my situation. Did they not see my face was being licked nearly down to the bone? I swatted at the beast, hysterical: "Get it off! *Get it off!*"

Finally, somebody took the dog by the collar and shooed it from me. It trotted happily away, tail swishing the air like a fly swatter. Scared and embarrassed, I began sobbing.

My mom bent down, assuring me the dog had meant no harm. "It's okay," she said. "He was just happy to see you."

She could say whatever she wanted. I knew a mauling when I felt one. "I want to go home," I choked. "I want to go *hooooooome!*"

My poor parents, with three children under the age of six, probably hadn't had a night out in months. Maybe longer. Here, finally, was an opportunity for them to be among other adults, and their "sensitive" child was threatening to ruin the evening before it even began.

I remember planting myself on the floor and shrieking to get my way. As a middle child sandwiched between an older brother and a sister with demanding medical needs, I felt no compunctions about throwing the occasional fit to be heard. My high-pitched screams must have been annoying to the adults, but I hope they blew out the eardrums of that fucking dog.

We were now drawing attention. Faceless grown-ups gathered in a semicircle around our family as my mom tried to soothe me, my dad just behind her, that familiar sheepish smile on his face. Finally, I heard a male voice reach across the thrum of adult murmurings and say, not unkindly, "C'mon . . . be a man."

I'd never heard that phrase before, but I understood exactly what he meant: not only was I behaving like a baby, but I was acting like a *girl* baby, the worst kind of baby I could be. An immediate and awful shame washed over me, humiliation now mixing with my terror.

I started crying harder. "I . . . want . . . to . . . go . . . home," I sputtered.

We didn't stay long.

The message—"be a man"—stuck with me. What exactly did he mean? What exactly was I supposed to do to be a man? First and foremost, I suppose he wanted me to shut up. I get it. When you were that age and threw your own fits over what appeared, to my adult eyes, to be innocuous events, I wanted the same from you. So much of parenting young children is simply trying to persuade them to stop screaming.

So, does "being a man" mean "being quiet"? In a certain way, yeah. One of the first things we learn about being men is that we're expected to suffer in silence. Actually, we're not really supposed to suffer at all. Whatever pain we experience is meant to be handled with minimal fuss. All the better if we can just grit our teeth and bear it.

Oddly, though, while men are meant to be stoic and quiet, boys are meant to be boisterous and loud. So while "being a man" indicates a certain amount of restraint, "boys will be boys" suggests wild abandon.

When I was growing up, the boys who ran around yelling, wrestling, and beating each other with tree branches were looked upon with approval or, at worst, bemused tolerance. Loud boys were thought to exhibit good manly behaviors like aggression and competitiveness. Quiet boys were viewed with some suspicion. They were seen as passive and submissive, qualities that were thought to be feminine (and therefore bad).

It's weird—nobody ever tells a girl to "be a woman." They might tell her to "be a lady," but never a woman. Being a lady implies behaving with a decorum not demanded of girls. Every girl experiences a moment when she is first shamed into behaving in a more "ladylike" fashion. A lady is some elegant, traditionally feminine ideal. Ladies don't lick the bottoms of their ice cream bowls, for example, even when there is no other way to slurp up the last dregs.

Being a *woman*, though, has an almost entirely different meaning. Ladies attend balls and sup with the queen. They sit demurely on the divan sipping sherry while men gather in the drawing room to talk business. Women, though, are active. Women do women's work, scrubbing floors and cooking meals. Ladies offer their gentlemen callers a peck on the cheek after a night at the theater. Ladies are chaste; women have sex. I hate to be so blunt about it, but it's the truth. We associate womanhood with sexual maturity instead of emotional maturity in a way that we don't with men and manhood. That's why the hallmark of a girl's early passage into womanhood is when she gets her first period. "You're a woman now," goes the popular (and cheesy) saying.

One of the strange things about parenting both a boy and a girl is realizing how early sexism starts. I used to tell a joke in my act about how when people met my infant son for the first time they'd tell me how handsome he was, etc. etc., but when they met my infant daughter for the first time, inevitably somebody would say, "She's going to be trouble." Which I always thought was weird because the trouble they were implying she was going to get into was sexual. They meant it as a compliment, I guess, but when they said, "She's going to be trouble," all I heard was, "She's going to suck a lot of dicks."

Girls are sexualized in a way that boys are not. Once

girls hit puberty, the culture begins treating their bodies as objects of fascination and desire. Those cultural cues don't just come from men, by the way. Open up any women's fashion magazine and look at the ads: Gucci, Dior, Versace, whatever. The clothes in those ads are all exorbitantly expensive: $1,700 blue jeans, $2,500 handbags—clothing practically no young woman can afford. But who's modeling it? Teenagers. The adult women who read these magazines are looking at aspirational photos of girls. The other ads in fashion magazines are for youth serums. It's perverse: girls are rushed into young adulthood and then asked to remain there, suspended in adolescent amber, for decades.

It's different with men. A boy's manhood is never assumed simply because of his biology. Yes, he will grow. Yes, he will enter puberty and emerge on the other side as a physical man, which is to say he will be bigger and stronger than a child and capable of reproduction. But his manhood—the qualities that distinguish him from a boy—will remain in doubt until he has somehow proven himself to be a man.

That's why the phrase "be a man" makes sense in a way that "be a woman" does not. A boy is thought to earn his manhood, whereas a girl's womanhood is primarily controlled by the passage of time. She will become a woman whether she wants to or not, but a boy may remain, in a sense, a boy well into adulthood. Adam Sandler built an entire career on that idea.

Even when achieved, manhood always feels conditional. Everything a man does or says is parsed to determine his continued worth as a man, all of it measured against a standard of manliness arbitrated by everybody and nobody. That measuring starts early, as early as a stranger telling a toddler terrorized by a dog to "be a man."

Boys grow up hearing these kinds of admonitions all the time.

"Be a man," we're told, which means, "Stop crying."

"Man up," we're told, which means, "Stop complaining."

"Act like a man," we're told, which means, "Stop expressing pain or fear."

When that guy told me to be a man, he wasn't asking me to be a man at all. He was asking me to be a certain kind of man because, to so many of us, only one model of manhood exists. When you deviate from it, you may find your masculinity attacked, which is to say you may feel as though your deepest self is being attacked. To say, "Be a man," is exactly the same as saying, "You are not a man."

In my case, that was true. I was a boy. Now I'm middle-aged, living in the woods with my wife and two kids. I've done lots of man things: grown up, slept around, worked hard, gotten married, raised children, buried my parents. I'm a man. No better or worse than any other. I know myself to be a man through biology, disposition, and experience. My sense of my own manhood snuck up on me without my even noticing. One day I didn't feel like a man and then I did. I didn't will myself into it any more than a tadpole wills itself into becoming a frog.

Nobody knows what "being a man" means because the model we've used to understand our roles as men is breaking down. Why? For a host of reasons, some of which are related to why our understanding of what it means to be a woman broke down in the 1960s.

Over the last half century or so, women have been working to redefine their roles in society. I can use the story of a friend of mine as a good example. She grew up in Stamford, Connecticut, in the '50s and early '60s. Her intellectual parents were supportive of her, but they never encouraged her to develop any of her interests into a career. She got married young, at age twenty, to her first boyfriend, Jeffrey, whom she met while she was still in high school. Her life as a young married woman was about following her husband as his career developed, first as a military pilot, then as he began working in the State Department.

One day around 1970, she says, Jeffrey came home from his job in Washington, D.C., and saw her on the couch watching the show *That Girl*, about a single woman living on her own—at the time a very modern and risqué premise. Seeing her there, Jeffrey told her she needed to find something to do with her life or she was going to be bored out of her mind. At the time, she says, it had never even occurred to her to have a career. "Jeffrey was the first feminist I ever met," she said.

She went back to school and got a college degree. After a short stint working on nuclear budgets in Washington, she saw an advertisement in the classified section of the newspaper. A little gourmet food store was for sale on Long Island. With Jeffrey's encouragement, she bought the store and kept its name, The Barefoot Contessa. Forty years later, Ina Garten is one of the most popular cookbook authors and television personalities in the world.

Ina's success is obviously unusual, but her story is a great illustration of the evolution of women's roles in a culture that was used to seeing them only as "happy" wives and mothers. The change was made possible by a revolutionary movement that initiated a conversation about what it means to be a woman—an often contentious conversation that continues to this day. The fundamental message of feminism, though, seems to have won out: girls can do anything and be anyone they wish to be.

(Some would add, "Except president of the United

States," though perhaps by the time this book is published, or shortly thereafter, that will no longer be true.)

That expansive message was designed to help women achieve equality with men. We can see the results. Girls are outperforming boys in school, graduating at higher rates from college, earning more money than ever before, and, as a result, living more autonomous lives. Although we haven't achieved anything near gender equality yet, the strides we've made in the last sixty years have been incredible.

You have no idea how different it is now even from when I was growing up in the '70s and '80s. Back then sexism in the workplace was so common, men couldn't even see it. The thought that a working woman should be taken as seriously as a man was, for a lot of guys, absurd. (If you want to see a hilarious take on this, watch *Anchorman*.)

It was so different for boys. As a kid, I certainly never felt that my sex would inhibit any dreams I might have. I could do anything, be anything. At the same time, there were other sorts of limits placed on the way I could live my life as a man that weren't true for the girls

I knew. Emotional limits, primarily. Even today, I bump up against them when I talk about issues related to men and masculinity, as if the act of even discussing those topics diminishes my own manhood. Whenever I post something critical about men on Twitter, for example, I'll almost always find myself getting trolled. Generally, I'll get a response like, "What would you know about being a man?"

I'm happy to take the bait. I tell them I obviously don't know as much they do. Could they tell me what it means? They struggle to reply. Most of the time, they'll tell me what being a man doesn't mean. Being a man does *not* mean "being a little bitch" or "a pussy." It doesn't mean, as I have been told, "acting like a faggot."

One troll told me I am not a "real man."

I asked him to define "real man."

"Not you," came the response.

But why not me? What about my manhood is any less real than his? One of the best aspects of modern feminism is the recognition that there are many ways to be a woman, as many different ways as there are women. A single woman who works on Wall Street is no less of a woman than a married stay-at-home mom out in the burbs. They may face different challenges related to their sex, but it would be hard to say that one of them is a "real" woman and one is not. The same isn't true for men; it wouldn't be unusual to hear somebody say that a hard-charging stockbroker is a "real man" but a stay-at-home dad is not.

Why? Why hasn't the conversation around manhood kept pace with the conversation around womanhood? Why don't we ever talk about the role of men in the culture except to point out our shortcomings? Perhaps because, to an overwhelming extent, men *are* the culture. It's only when the culture begins to change that men are forced to confront their own dominant place within it. That's what we see now. It's why we need a commensurate, positive message for men that mirrors the one women have led for the last half century.

As we start asking questions about ourselves, we begin to recognize that a lot of men's problems stem from a lack of understanding about who we are supposed to be in this evolving culture. That's why the

Twitter troll couldn't answer my question about what it means to be a "real man." He doesn't know. I don't blame him. I don't know, either—I only know my own experiences.

Here's what I can tell you about my experience of being a man. For one thing, it's a lot less dramatic than I thought it would be when I was a kid. Fewer karate battles, for one thing.

On the other hand, it's a richer experience than I expected. Its rewards are subtle and are tied to a defined sense of purpose and community. I feel it when we sit down to dinner as a family. When I kiss you good night even though you are eighteen and it annoys you. When I take your sister out for driving lessons and somehow manage to restrain myself from grabbing the steering wheel every few seconds. Manhood, or at least my manhood, is quiet and simple and straightforward. I'm not sure I have the right word to describe this feeling. The closest I can think of is "settledness," which I mean in the sense of being rooted in my place, the way a house settles into the earth.

I still have anxiety about the future, career worries, money worries, regrets. These concerns require attention and care, the same way a house requires attention and care. But my foundational sense of myself, the part that includes my being a guy, feels more secure than it ever has. In other words, I'm happy.

Happiness is a quality people rarely discuss when talking about what it means to be a man. Actually, the opposite seems true. Manhood is usually thought of as a grim business. Men endure. They sacrifice. They have "grit." All of which may be true to a certain extent, but equally true is that men also do silly dances, fold laundry, try out recipes. At least this man does. I feel like no less of a man when I'm happy playing piano (badly) than when I'm miserable shoveling snow off the walk.

Boys are taught that the institutions of manhood (work and, perhaps, fatherhood) will make us men. Manliness is the goal. This message is obviously flawed because it suggests that being seen as a man, in and of itself, is the mark of a life well lived. We aren't taught to question our roles, only to get on with the business of being men. There isn't a lot of room for self-reflection or self-doubt. Any disquiet we may feel is a flaw within ourselves, a blemish on our manhood.

Women experience deep conflict—sometimes internal, sometimes externally imposed—over their inability to "have it all." Men are supposed to already have it all. Traditional manhood does not allow space for unhappiness because happiness, or a lack thereof, is mostly irrelevant to the business of being a man. Instead, the measure of our manhood is our utility.

Do you remember that TV show you used to watch when you were little, *Thomas & Friends*, about a bunch of (mostly male) talking locomotives? The highest compliment they could receive was being a "really useful engine." That's the hinge on which traditional manhood swings. I'm not knocking it, by the way, since all people are at their best when they're in service to others. I'm just saying, there are times when being a useful engine may not be enough because even the best-made things sometimes break down. Sometimes, despite your best efforts, despite your attempts to suck it up without complaint, despite your manly stoicism, you break.

You fall. You may sometimes feel defeated. Traditional manhood doesn't give us the toolkit to deal with those moments. What do we do then? What do we do when we find ourselves plopped on the floor, sobbing to go home?

FIVE

No Sissy Stuff

Be Yourself

THERE'S AN OLD sketch from *Saturday Night Live* called *"¿Quién es Más Macho?"* The setting is a fake Venezuelan game show hosted by a mustachioed Bill Murray, in which the contestants are presented with a choice of two famous actors. Their task is to guess which of the two is more macho. The entire sketch is performed in Spanish, the most macho of languages. Here's some sample dialogue:

Bill Murray: *¿Quién es más macho? Fernando Lamas o Ricardo Montalbán.*
(You'll remember Ricardo Montalbán as the actor who played Khan in *Star Trek*. I have no

idea who Fernando Lamas was, but I'm sure he was a total stud.)

Jorge, a contestant, rings in.

Jorge: *¿Ricardo Montalbán?*

A buzzer sounds.

Bill Murray: *No, es falso. Fernando Lamas es un poquito más macho.*

What makes the sketch funny is the idea that there's a correct answer to such an obviously subjective (and silly) question. And yet, somehow, in the complicated language of masculinity, Fernando Lamas *is* a little more macho than Ricardo Montalbán.

Women speak the language of masculinity, too, much more fluently than men speak the language of femininity, for the same reason that more Latvians speak Russian than Russians speak Latvian. The dominant power will always impose its culture on the subservient power. In the male/female relationship, men have always been the dominant power, so women have had to learn the ways of men to protect themselves. That's why men always think women are so "mysterious." Bullshit. Women are no more mysterious than Latvians: we just haven't troubled ourselves to learn their language.

As boys get older, we learn that everything we say or do as a male—literally every single thing—can be assigned a spot on an Infinite Axis of Manliness. These verbal and nonverbal cues, when taken together, assign you a rank. The rank is how your manliness measures up against that of every other man.

I'll pick a random example from my life to illustrate:

As I write these words, I've got a steaming mug of hot tea beside me, the same tea you see me drinking every morning. I can easily break down the experience of drinking this tea into its components and rank all of them on the Infinite Axis of Manliness.

¿Quién es más macho? Coffee or tea?

Coffee *es más macho* for reasons that go back to the founding of our country. According to food historian Tori Avey, although coffee was available in America before the Revolution, "the drink wasn't really popular in America until the Boston Tea Party of 1773, when making the switch from tea to coffee became something of a patriotic duty." Tea's reputation never recovered. Since then, tea has been associated with a kind of effete European aristocracy. The thing is, I don't like coffee. It's too bitter and it gets me jittery. So I drink tea. My tea drinking is one data point along the Infinite Axis.

Another strike against me: I like a splash of milk in my tea. Any nonalcoholic addition to a beverage automatically makes it less masculine. Black coffee *es muy macho*. Worse, the milk I choose is 2 percent fat, which is so much less masculine than whole milk because whole milk has a higher fat content, but at the same time it is somehow *more* masculine than half-and-half. Why? Because half-and-half used to be seen as a healthier alternative to full cream. Any dietary choice a man makes for "health reasons" is less masculine than a dietary choice that does not take health into consideration. A Real Man doesn't care about his health because worrying about superficial shit like heart disease suggests that you're afraid of dying. Nothing scares a Real Man, least of all death.

Back to tea: Caffeinated is more masculine than

decaffeinated. Tea without sugar is more masculine than tea with sugar because the taste profile "sweet" is less masculine than the taste profile "bitter." Women drink sweet things. Men drink paint thinner.

I could go on and on: Sipping tea is less masculine than gulping. The size of the mug I choose, the design on the mug, the way I hold that mug—by the handle or cupped from below? Pinky out or pinky in? Coaster or no? Do I wipe my mouth with a napkin or with my shirtsleeve?

You could pluck anything from your life and do this same exercise. The way you sit, the way you sleep, the books you read (Civil War history, yes; Victorian literature, no). The foods you eat, the car you drive, the words you choose. I used to—and sometimes still do— get teased because I had a larger vocabulary than some of my peers. A C student is somehow more macho than an A student.

George W. Bush won the presidency partially by embracing his own "regular guy" intellectual mediocrity. During a commencement speech at Yale, he said, "To those of you who received honors, awards and distinctions, I say well done. And to the C students, I say, you, too, can be president of the United States."

He said the line with good humor, and it was funny, but the truth is that his joke also served a larger, destructive narrative about "intellectuals," that they are somehow less authentic than the C students of the world. Years later, Donald Trump would get cheers when he declared, "I love the poorly educated." Being smart *no es muy macho*.

Here's another presidential example that still boggles my mind. You won't remember this because you were too young, but when Barack Obama first became president, he and Vice President Joe Biden did a little PR thing where they went to a local burger joint for lunch. All very fine and manly. But then, the president did the unthinkable: he asked for Dijon mustard on his cheeseburger.

Obama, you fool! Dijon mustard *no es macho*! Why? Because it's a French mustard and all true American men know that the French are a race of handkerchief-waving dandies, their expertise with the guillotine notwithstanding. French culture—indeed *all* culture—has taken on a suspicious cast in recent decades, a fear that a world of beauty is a threat to the world of brawn. Dijon mustard, as an idea, hits a metaphorical sweet spot for a certain mindset that would view a sandwich condiment as a threat to American manhood.

Fox News actually aired a sneering story about the U.S. President's choice of mustard. They ran a chyron for that segment which screamed in all caps: PRESIDENT ASKS FOR DIJON MUSTARD ON HIS BURGER AT LOCAL DINER.

The host of the show, a ceramic pig named Sean Hannity, began by sarcastically intoning, "As you all know, President Barack Obama is a real man of the people." He then belittled the president for more than a minute over his choice of condiments, ending the segment by saying, "I hope you enjoyed that *fancy* burger, Mr. President."

To be "fancy" is to be cultured, educated, elitist . . . and feminine.

Filtered through the cyclotron of stupidity known as Fox News, President Obama's mustard became an indictment against his masculinity, furthering a narrative they were building about his lack of "toughness" and, therefore, his lack of fitness to serve as president.

Insane.

Yet every man understood exactly what Hannity was driving at because we're all fluent in the language of masculinity. We learn it along with our ABC's. According to a study conducted by City University in London, by age three, most kids know whether they are a boy or girl, and by four they have a "stable sense of gender identity," meaning they know the stuff that "boys do" and the stuff that "girls do."

The nuances come later, of course, but now that you are grown, you are surely more than capable of distilling who among us is a Real Man and who is not. So I'll ask you: *¿Quién es más macho?* Firemen or factory workers? Teachers or tax preparers? The lacrosse player or the kid on the chess team? The committed husband or the committed bachelor? The guy who bottles up his emotions or the one who risks ridicule by expressing them?

We can't answer these questions in a satisfactory

way, yet our whole notion of masculinity is predicated on trying to do exactly that. Which is why forty years ago, you got Bill Murray spoofing it on an episode of *Saturday Night Live*. And it's why, unfortunately, the sketch is still funny today.

Traditional masculinity is an elaborate system of ritualized posturing. A kind of drag show. It's men in carefully assembled attire lip-synching the songs of their fathers and grandfathers. At their most grandiose, both drag shows and displays of traditional masculinity are campy exhibitions of gender blown out to cartoonish proportions. The only difference is that drag performers have a sense of humor. Sometimes I think the only thing separating RuPaul and Chuck Norris is glitter.

It's easy enough for me to see that now, easy enough for me to explain it to you. It would've been tough, though, to lay that out for a kid like me growing up in 1980s New Jersey. My little town, Hillsborough, had been an agricultural community until five minutes before we moved there, when townhouse developments like mine began sprouting up like mushrooms. It attracted mostly young boomer families, clean white collars replacing overalls. A new supermarket went in, a McDonald's, an upscale mall called Bridgewater Commons. The high school got an extension. Everything felt fast and cheap and dumb, a town without a community. They were building a workforce there, an assembly line churning out the future mid-level managers of America. I wanted no part of it.

I knew that the life I wanted to live for myself, a life of creative exploration, wouldn't be possible for me there. Even the concept of "creativity" was frowned upon for boys; boys who took too many art classes, for example, were suspect. The same was true for boys who performed in the school plays, or sang in the choir, or those who played "female" instruments like the flute.

Yes, there are "female" instruments because—remember—*everything* can be ranked along the Infinite Axis. Instruments such as the flute or piccolo, which are small and in the higher range, are considered more feminine than instruments like the tuba, which are heavier and in the lower range. Besides the brawn required to lug them around, I assume the perception has something to do with the way their timbres are associated with the human voice. Drums are the most masculine because they involve hitting stuff.

Actually, as I'm writing this, I'm remembering that when we had to choose instruments to learn in fifth grade, I actually *wanted* to play the flute because I liked the weird, sideways way they were held. My mom dissuaded me, saying that the flute rental was too expensive. But, she said, she could afford the clarinet. Why would the flute cost any more to rent than the clarinet?

She didn't seem to have any problem affording my brother's saxophone. It's only now, writing this down, that I realize the reason my mom didn't want me to play the flute was because she didn't want the other kids to think I was gay. Keep in mind, this is my gay mom worrying about her younger son's sexuality. She knew the language of gender as well as anybody. Probably better than most. For boys, the first rule, as Deborah S. David and Robert Brannon wrote in their 1976 book about male gender roles, *The Forty-Nine Percent Majority*, is simple: "No sissy stuff."

The insult "sissy" has fallen out of favor but I actually think it's the best one we've got to describe the squishy center of male anxiety. To be thought as a sissy is to be laughable, dismissible, irrelevant. Barely worthy of scorn. In the hierarchy of traditional manhood, a sissy is less than a woman because he inhabits no purposeful space. He is a non-male. He's nothing.

By the time I grew up, "sissy" had fallen out of favor, replaced with the harder-edged "faggot," a word that leaned more heavily on sexuality. Sissies were suspect, but faggots were a threat. My early adolescence coincided with the height of gay panic. The gay rights movement and the AIDS crisis were coming of age together. There were news stories nearly every day about gay people: marching, dying, demanding—some of them were even kissing in public, for God's sake! Suddenly, homosexuality seemed to be everywhere. In towns like mine all over the country, boys who didn't fit into the neat box of traditional masculinity, regardless of their sexuality, were looked at with deep suspicion, even fear.

Tom Waits has that song about paranoia, in which a neighbor is working on something in his garage and the narrator of the song just keeps asking, "What's he building in there?" as if the answer could only be something nefarious. That's kind of what it felt like back then growing up as a boy who didn't quite fit the ready-made mold of boyhood. What was I building in there? I couldn't have told them because I didn't know myself.

Perhaps it's less true for your generation—I'd like to think so—but my generation equated masculinity with sexuality. Whatever other attributes a guy had were knocked down to nothing if he also happened to be gay. A guy's sexuality overrode anything else the world saw about him as a man. Being gay was the lowest place you could occupy on the Infinite Axis, which was why it was such a big deal when gay men starting coming out of the closet. They were risking everything, even in some cases their lives, by making themselves visible to a world that refused to see them.

I now think: What could be more macho than that?

The concept of "gender fluidity" was unknown to us then, aside from some dim awareness that some people liked to wear the clothing of the opposite sex. Once a year, my high school held a powder-puff football game, in which girls would take the field to play a rowdy match of touch football. The varsity football team would dress up as cheerleaders for the event, donning skirts and wigs and makeup, stuffing their sweaters with big wads of paper towels to make breasts. The fact that this was "hilarious" is a testament to our rigid adherence to strict gender codes. Years later, one of the biggest guys on the team came out as gay. I wonder what he made of powder-puff football.

As a kid, one of the few things I knew about myself was my sexuality. I've known I was straight since the first time I fell in love, at four, with a neighborhood girl named Sarah. Innumerable crushes followed, all of them straight, most of them unrequited.

Even so, part of my confusion about gender involved recognizing from a young age that I did, indeed, enjoy "sissy" stuff. Yes, I liked the hard play of boyhood, running around and yelling and spinning donuts on my push-pedal Big Wheel. But I also liked quieter, "girlish" activities like reading and role-playing and whispering secrets. I liked hanging out with girls as much as boys, often more so. I liked baseball and musical theater and building forts in the woods and writing little stories. I liked playing pretend.

From a fairly young age, maybe eight or nine, I sensed that I couldn't be my full self without judgment. Kids pick up on slight differences between them. They tease one another, poke and prod and try to get under your skin. What was wrong with carrying myself the way I carried myself, expressing myself the way I did? Why did it feel like such a chore to just move through the day as myself? And if it was happening to me, it must have been happening to so many other kids as well. Some of them like me, some of them with the opposite problem: everybody assumed they were straight but they knew themselves to be gay. Maybe they felt misgendered. Maybe they didn't know and didn't understand why their sexuality or gender expression mattered to anybody but themselves. Maybe they understood the maddening dilemma of trying to fit in with the group while also being themselves. Why did those two things have to be in conflict?

If a man is willing to accept the premise that he must conform to a model of behavior that allows him to be a man, then what else is he agreeing to? What other pacts is he making in order to ensure his place within his culture? And why? Every person craves acceptance in their group. Groups play by rules. Breaking the rules risks losing one's place in the group. When rules become too hidebound, however, they eventually squeeze the life out of the thing they're meant to protect.

Author Michael Chabon wrote a terrific essay about this idea in his book *Pops: Fatherhood in Pieces*. Chabon received a magazine assignment to cover the Paris fashion shows, and he allowed his fashion-obsessed teenage son to tag along. The son spent the week hanging out with a bunch of designers and fashionistas, and when it came time to leave, he was disconsolate. Chabon misunderstood, thinking the teen had enjoyed the fashion shows and meeting cool people, and was reluctant to return to his humdrum life. But it wasn't that, the boy insisted. It was something else.

Chabon finally realized that his son had been dressing himself in elaborate clothes and costumes for years not because he was "trying to prove how different he was from everyone else." He'd been doing it "in the hope of attracting the attention of somebody else— somewhere, someday—who was the *same*." The essay ends with this beautiful observation:

> "You were with your people. You found them," I said.
> He nodded.
> "That's good," I said. "You're early."

The enduring image I have from your childhood is the way you used to sit in the backseat when we took car trips, your blankie cradled under your arm, thumb in mouth, watching the world flicker past the window. You never complained, never kicked the back of the seat, rarely fell asleep. When I glanced into the rearview mirror, there you were, attending to the world as you found it, content.

You've always seemed at ease with yourself. I don't

know where you got that from because I certainly never had it. Neither did Mom. We were both restless kids, both of us wanting something we couldn't name, something we knew we'd have to find away from home.

When I was a kid, I felt like I watched so many of the boys (and girls) around me move along the conveyor belt without ever considering their destination. It was easier that way. I was lucky, I guess, that I felt alienated, because it forced me to think about alternative ways to express myself, alternative dreams to chase, alternative ideas of the person I could become. I envy the ease you have with yourself, but I am grateful for my own itchiness.

For all of its tough talk and false bravado, traditional masculinity is so easily spooked by boys who want to live outside of its narrow boundaries. "No sissy stuff" isn't really about femininity; it's about control. We learn to control ourselves, but in doing so, we also become objects of that control. Traditional masculinity tries to keep men on as narrow a path as possible. When you deviate from it, it pushes you back.

I look at you and I see a classic straight white male. You wear hoodies and T-shirts with funny sayings and the same scuffed sneakers we bought you two years ago. Whenever Mom asks if you need any new clothes or, really, anything at all, you tell us you're good, that you've got everything you need. Maybe you do and maybe you don't. Sometimes, I see the gears of your brain turning in quiet clicks, and I wonder—what are you building in there?

As we open the door for you and usher you into the next part of your life, I hope you bring your natural comfort with you. I also hope you let it go. Once in a while, seek out the stuff that scares you and move in that direction. It's that stuff, whatever it winds up being, that will offer you the most rewards. In a weird way, our masculinity holds us back from walking toward our fears because, although it preaches bravery and strength, it doesn't allow for the possibility that we won't be brave, that we won't be strong. It doesn't allow us to reach out to others for support in our times of fear. That's what "no sissy stuff" tells us.

I'm encouraging you to look for the stuff that makes you uncomfortable because that's the stuff that will end up mattering the most. Allow yourself to be frightened, to flounder around, and to fail. Let yourself lose control, reach out, let others pull you up. The ones who do will be your people. Find your people.

SIX

Do You Even Lift, Bro?

Share the Load

THE OTHER DAY, I called a friend who I heard was going through a hard time.

"Hey, man," I said.

"Hey."

"How's it going?"

"Good, good," he answered. (He wasn't good.) "How're you?"

"Good!" (I was so-so.)

We chatted for a few minutes about what each of us was doing with our days, cracking jokes, studiously avoiding what we both knew to be the purpose of the call, that he was in emotional crisis, and that I was reaching out to him. Mom watched me conduct my end of the conversation with a combination of awe and horror.

"What did he say?"

I shrugged.

"How is he?"

"He seemed okay."

You and I have had similar conversations when I've asked you about school, girls, your life. Shrugs, silence. Teenage omertà is nothing new, especially among boys, but I wish it didn't have to be so.

Ruthie, sixteen, also suffers our questions in silence, but she wears her emotions on her sleeve. We may not know the specifics of whatever she's going through at any given moment, but we get a sense. You, on the other hand, are impenetrable, almost Zen in your stillness. Everything is always fine. When I press, you joke away my questions or change the subject. It's not that I'm worried about you now, exactly, it's that I'm worried about what you will do when things aren't fine because I know what it costs when you don't let others in.

If the first rule of manhood is "No sissy stuff," the second is "Suck it up."

Psychologist and author Jordan Peterson has built an enormous following by instructing his (mostly white, mostly male) acolytes that the purpose of life is to "pick up your suffering and bear it."

Pain will come, he is saying, and when it does, nobody wants to hear about it. Why should your pain be any more deserving of our attention than anybody else's? Bear your pain, he says in one lecture, "so when your father dies you are not whining away in the corner and you can help plan the funeral."

At my father's funeral, I sat in the front row with my hands folded on my lap. Later, at the burial site, I watched them lower the coffin into the ground. On the way back, I sat with my head against the window, just the way you used to do on long car trips. After a few days, I went back to school and pretended nothing had happened. I got through it. I didn't whine.

Having tried Peterson's method for most of my life, I can tell you it only works as a tourniquet. You may get through the moment, the day, the week. Eventually though, the blood stops flowing altogether, and something in you falls away.

Peterson doesn't confine his philosophy to men, but his appeal is mostly limited to them. And no wonder. His advice confirms what most of us have been told our entire lives. Peterson is the first to admit his idea isn't new. Buddhism's First Noble Truth is that life contains suffering. All religions acknowledge this. Any human who has ever lived will say the same. What they don't agree on is what to do about it.

I cannot recall the number of times I wiped tears from your face when you were little. I can remember the feeling of your pudgy arms around my neck as I knelt down to you, listening to you stammer out the reasons for your pain, holding you until you felt better, wiping your snot off my shirt. Coming to me for comfort was one of the greatest gifts you ever gave to me because it allowed me to be your dad. A dad instructs and reprimands and plays. I've done all those things, too, but comforting you felt special, the gift of extending empathy. I don't know why it felt so unexpectedly good to share your pain. Maybe because I was able to give you something my dad never gave me; I can't remember a single hug. Sharing your pain with me relieved my own terror of fathering a son. In allowing me to comfort you, you comforted me.

When my mom died a couple years ago, I wanted to experience her loss. I knew that I did not allow myself to grieve for my father when he died, and that failing to do so had condemned me to years of excommunication from my own emotional life. For my mom, I wanted to live my mourning instead of hiding from it. I didn't exactly know what that meant, didn't know exactly how I would mourn other than to try to be present for whatever happened and to let whatever felt true be okay.

I got on a plane by myself and flew to San Diego, where Mom had lived with her lovely partner, Sandy. For three days, I folded and unfolded collapsible chairs, cleaned pastry crumbs from counters. I sat shiva and thanked people for coming and reminisced with my brother, and with Sandy and her family. I did all the things I was expected to do, dry-eyed and composed. No whining. Numb. Angry with myself for my numbness. As I left Mom and Sandy's apartment at the end of those three days, I felt like I had failed to even mourn the way I wanted. I had lived with the tourniquet for so long I didn't know how to release it.

That night, I came back to my hotel room and, after a couple hours of drinking, collapsed in tears on the floor, alone. I wish I'd had the strength to share my hurt in front of other people, and I wish it hadn't taken half a bottle of vodka for me to do so then.

I talk about my mom a lot, sharing stories of my love for her, yes, but also trying to sort through the conflicting emotions I have for a woman who did so many things right when raising us, and so many things wrong. The tears were not an endpoint to my grief, they were a beginning. I hate Peterson's advice because I have seen how an unrelieved burden can cripple a boy; I've seen how asking for help can empower a man.

Yet my instinct is still to muscle through difficult moments by myself when I could use a hand. I still do everything in my power to keep my pain from showing. Most of the time, I think it's entirely appropriate to keep a stiff upper lip, to endure scrapes and bruises with good cheer and "tut-tut" and all of that. But I also think it's necessary to expel some of that hurt at times, to bleed on the carpet.

I keep seeing myself, alone, on that flight to San Diego. Why didn't I bring you guys with me to say goodbye to Grandma Jill? I've asked myself that time and again. Fear, I think, fear of being so exposed in front of my kids. How stupid. How disrespectful to her and to you. How utterly, baldly stupid. I'm sorry.

"Suck it up" runs so deep in men. We learn it young and we learn it often. I had a conversation with a woman over email who told me a story about her father and brother. She comes from a family of three, two girls and a boy.

Their dad was gentle with his girls. Not so with the son. Once, when they were children, her brother was given some medication he couldn't swallow. It's a common problem with kids—they're afraid to swallow pills because they think they're going to choke. Her father grew irate: "My little brother sat on a washing machine while my dad forced his hands down my brother's throat, screaming, *'Be a man!'* I witnessed this five-year-old boy crying and vomiting everywhere—my brother couldn't swallow his pills and my dad was furious."

She told me this kind of behavior was common, saying he "constantly abused and violently hurt my brother for years."

Later in life, the brother tried to kill himself several times. She thinks it was, in large part, a result of the abuse he suffered at the hands of their father. But when she talks about her dad she has sympathy for him, saying he wasn't "a bad man," but that instead, "He did the best he knew how . . . the way his father had taught him, and so on."

I suspect that, more often than not, when fathers hurt their sons it's an expression of their own terrors. In a perverse way, they're trying to prepare their boys for a world that will treat them even more harshly than they did. Be strong, they're saying, because the weak do not survive.

Strength is a man's chief weapon against the world, the quality that keeps his fear at bay. Strength is protection and comfort and hope. There are, of course, many kinds of strength but they all serve the same purpose. It is the way we assert our place in the world and keep it. The first type of strength we think of is physical strength. It's often the first thing men compare about each other. I have no empirical evidence to back this up, but I suspect guys find ourselves subconsciously sizing each other up. We don't mean to. We don't want to. But our male conditioning has trained us to ask ourselves the familiar primal question: *Could I take him?* I will admit to you right now, in my case the answer is always no.

I mean, do you even lift, bro?

As a boy, I remember comparing my own size and strength to my father's and feeling as though I would never measure up. How could I possibly expect to ever reach my father's otherworldly height of five feet and eight inches? Would I ever be able to, as he did, open a new jar of vacuum-sealed salsa with minimal strain and cursing? A child can imagine almost anything, but I found it hard to imagine I would ever be stronger than my father, a man who probably could not have mustered more than ten decent push-ups.

To me, though, he was strong. As strong as any man. All fathers must seem incomparably mighty to their young children. Even I, twiggy as I am, felt the wonder of my own strength with you guys when you were little. I loved picking you up and carrying you under my arm like a gym bag, or swinging you onto my shoulders and parading you around like a maharaja.

Strength like that is great but fleeting. You are already stronger than me, as you should be. You're eighteen, I'm not. I want to encourage you, though, to flip the idea of strength on its head. There will be times when your deepest strength will come not from showing how much pain you can endure, but from allowing yourself to show that you are vulnerable.

In his lectures, Jordan Peterson sometimes equates his philosophy with the example set by Jesus picking up his cross and carrying it, alone, through the Via Dolorosa. It's a powerful image, the son of God silently enduring his torture; his body may be hurt, but his spirit cannot be punctured. Until it is. And here is where, to me, Peterson's argument falls apart. On the cross, Jesus finally succumbs to his pain, calling out to his father:

"My God, my God, why have you forsaken me?" In that raw, agonizing moment he fully sheds his divinity and becomes one of us. Giving voice to suffering does not make you less of a man. It makes you more of a human.

We think of strength—all forms of strength—as a possession: either I *am* strong or I *am not* strong. Maybe that's a misapprehension. Maybe it's better to think of strength as a kind of common trust, something we hold for a time and then pass around like a library book. Each of us has the ability to borrow strength when needed; Mom and I do it all the time. When I'm feeling sorry for myself about a job I didn't get, or experiencing some seasonal malaise, or find myself growing anxious about the future, I lean on her. She does the same with me when she's dealing with her own regrets and anxieties. Leaning on each other keeps both of us upright.

Of course, this doesn't happen just in marriage. Family, friends, community: those are our true strengths. If we are strong, it is because, over and over again, others have used their own muscles to make us so. And we, in turn, do the same for them. It's an old idea—community—maybe just as old as "might makes right," but it's at odds with the way we think about men as rugged, self-sufficient individuals.

Yes, you should be strong in the ways that people are strong. Yes, you should persevere. You should endure. You should summon from yourself the most that you have to give, and you should give as much of yourself as you are able when you are able. These ideas are deeply embedded in traditional masculinity. But that vision of masculinity falters at the place where strength fails. That's the place where I am most interested in helping you because that's the place where I think guys need the most help.

There will be times in your life when you are not strong enough. When you do not know what else to do, where to turn; when you feel like you have given everything you can give. This is the moment where I want you to know that it's okay to reach out a hand and allow others to pick you up. I want your sister to know this, too: how and when to persevere, and when to ask for help. Women struggle with this issue just as much as men. Their upbringing so often conditions them to always offer a hand, but rarely to ask for one. If the projection of masculinity relies on the projection of strength, asking for help can be seen as admitting weakness. The three most difficult words for a guy to say are not "I love you." The three most difficult words for a guy to say are "I need help."

Allowing others to help us is just as important as offering help. This is a gift of our humanity, to give love and to allow others to give you their love. You can plan a funeral and mourn and whine all at the same time. You can be there for a friend on the phone. We all carry burdens. They will weigh us down and we will struggle with them, as we all must. It's okay to reach out for a hand when you are climbing a steep hill or to ask another to sit with you to rest for a while. We're strong, all of us. And, sometimes, we're weak. All of us. Your vulnerabilities reveal you. Let them. When you don't admit weakness, you close yourself off from receiving the strength of others, which is another way of saying you close yourself off from love. Instead, you twist the tourniquet a little bit tighter. You grow numb. Trust me. I spent most of my life that way.

Looking back on it now, though, I wonder why. Why is it so important for men to keep their guard up? What are we protecting? Why should our entire sex be forever primed for battle? Why do we sacrifice the hearts of boys?

✦✦✦✦

SEVEN

Beer from a Leg

Respect the Service of Others

WE USED TO take family vacations when I was a kid. Six people crammed into a two-tone green Pontiac Grand Prix. Hours upon hours of driving, Mom and Elaine's crappy country music blaring from the AM dial. Every few hours we'd stop at a roadside picnic table to eat soggy ham sandwiches and sip warm soda from paper cups.

Mom and Elaine always included an "educational element" on these excursions, some boring stop at some boring place where boring stuff happened a long time ago: Plymouth Rock, Colonial Williamsburg, Gettysburg. As a kid, I didn't see how any of these places had any relevance to my life aside from whatever candies they sold in their gift shops.

Gettysburg, in particular, was a snooze. They had a few cool cannons scattered about, and a gaudy monument memorializing the dead, but mostly it was a vast expanse of green, no more interesting to me than the farmers' fields within a walk of our townhouse. I kicked at the grass, hoping I'd uncover an old sword or something, but all I found was dirt.

The soldiers at Gettysburg fought over three days in July of 1863. Accounts from just after the battle talk about the field being covered with the bodies of the dead and wounded for miles around. A nurse named Cornelia Hancock describes the "sickening, overpowering, awful stench" from "dead bodies . . . lying in heaps on every side." Between them, the two armies suffered a total of about 50,000 casualties; it took a week to clear the corpses from the field for burial. What kind of strength must it have taken to endure those three days? It seems superhuman to me. Yet they were just guys, no different than you or me. Most of them weren't professional soldiers; they were farmers, students, merchants. Men and boys sent to war.

It was, and remains, America's worst war. We'd been a nation for only four score and seven years, yet we'd already been in about two dozen armed conflicts. Overseas, Europe was in a state of near perpetual conflict, as were Asia, the Middle East, and Africa. All over the globe, men were killing each other, just as they had been for thousands of years. The killing would continue into the twentieth century and, now, into the twenty-first. Human history has mostly been a series of wars interrupted by occasional bursts of baby making.

War, and the threat of war, has been our default setting for so long that we've oriented an entire gender around it. To make war, you need soldiers. To make soldiers, you need men.

Women have also fought in wars since there have been wars, but their numbers have always been few. For all of recorded human history, it's mainly been men marching back and forth across continents in the service of God and king, killing their enemies, taking what they wanted, however they wanted, burning the rest. In his remarkable book, *War and Gender*, Joshua S. Goldstein, professor emeritus of international relations at American University, writes, "Of the most warlike societies [ever] known, none requires women to participate in combat, and in all of them cultural concepts of masculinity motivate men to fight."

Those "cultural concepts" are key. When we emphasize aggression, strength, discipline, and pride in boys, we do so specifically because these exact qualities produce the best soldiers. When we de-emphasize empathy, creative thinking, self-expression, it's because these qualities are not as desirable in soldiers. This is why we sacrifice the hearts of boys; it's how we make soldiers.

We feed our soldiers words like "honor" to justify the pain they cause and "sacrifice" to ennoble the pain they endure. We suppress, or even erase, their empathy. We elevate the cause of the nation above the suffering of its people and above the suffering of the people they fight. We elevate the ones best able to do these things as "heroes" and cast out, imprison, or kill the ones who are unwilling to perform these functions: those men are called "traitors" and "cowards." Societies have often presented a stark choice to their nation's boys and men: Assume your responsibilities as men and fight with us, or be removed from us. Be a soldier or be nothing. No sacrifice is too great to bear in order to secure the nation.

Sometimes, as a kid, I'd lie awake wondering what I would do if I were ever asked to fight for my country. My main frame of reference for war back then was World War II, that noble campaign of the previous generation. Would I have gone? Yes, I thought. I would have volunteered, first in line to serve. Would I be brave? I thought I would be, yes. I would be the one to charge the Nazi machine gun nest, the one to jump on the grenade to save my buddies. Even when I was nine and ten years old, I knew I would never be the biggest boy, or the strongest. But I thought I could be brave.

It's funny: I never doubted my own bravery despite all evidence to the contrary. I should have known I was not cut out for heroics when the kisses of a neighbor's dog crumpled me to the floor in terror. I have rarely been brave. Given the opportunity to stand up to bullies, I have usually demurred. When push came to shove, more often than not, I simply stepped aside.

As I got older, I started mistaking snarkiness for bravery. In high school, I was quick with a snide remark, usually directed at the cool kids or the teachers or anybody to whom I felt inferior, which was everybody. I thought my jokes made me brave, but even then I knew I was risking nothing when I spouted off. There was no upside to kicking the ass of a scrawny kid like me. I could say what I wanted because nobody felt threatened by my doing so. My only weapon was my mouth. It was a peashooter.

Once, during my senior year of high school, our local army recruiter called the house while some friends were over. The local recruiters called every high school senior boy to ask if we'd thought about enlisting. Usually I just said no and ended the conversation, but this time I decided to fuck with him.

"I might be interested in enlisting," I said to him over the phone. "What kinds of opportunities are there in the army for musical theater actors?"

"Oh, many opportunities," he lied.

"That sounds very exciting," I said. "Would being gay affect my chances of promotion?" This was when gay people weren't allowed to serve, and if they discovered that you were gay, they kicked you out. The recruiter hemmed and hawed at my question as my friends stifled their laughter in the background. We weren't laughing at gay people; we were laughing at his obvious discomfort. I hung up on him.

It all felt like a joke to me. It wasn't. Only a couple years later, the United States amassed an army and went to war in Iraq. When the first bombs fell, I was in San Antonio laid up with the flu while touring the country as a Teenage Mutant Ninja Turtle, my first paid acting job. The boy who'd been so sure of his own bravery had a job dressing up in a very different uniform from the one worn by his peers in a faraway desert. I felt small and stupid as I watched the war on TV, and I felt very glad not to be there.

I was more than happy to let others stand in my place, and I knew who many of those others were: poor kids, minority kids, boys looking for discipline, or a way out of bad circumstances, boys from military families who walked the path of their fathers. Mostly boys with few other options. Back then, I didn't think of myself as especially privileged; I certainly didn't think I had come from much. But that was another lie I told myself.

After Dad died, I had life insurance money. Not a lot, but enough to get me through college. I could dismiss military service because I never had to give it serious consideration. A lot of other guys my age didn't have that choice. Duty had seemed so simple when I was a kid: when summoned, you went to war. When I was old enough to actually volunteer my service, though, I found it more prudent to watch the bombs go boom from the downy comfort of a hotel bed.

There's that line from *Henry IV Part I*, "The better part of valour is discretion." Perhaps, but discretion is a luxury a lot of young American men can't afford. Enlisting may be their ticket to college, a career, a handhold on the middle class. For many, their choice isn't between discretion and valor, but discretion and opportunity.

I remember driving over to the post office after I

turned eighteen to register for the draft, as required by law. There's no drama in filling out a form. You give the government information they already possess and wait for a letter you hope never comes. In doing so, you fulfill the barest duty of your citizenship as a man of this country. It's a transaction, no more.

You turned eighteen months ago. I picked up a form for you when Mom and I were out the other week, but it's just been sitting, ignored, on the counter. I keep reminding you that you have to fill it out. "I will," you say.

I don't press the issue.

That first Iraq War was over in about a month. Around 380 Americans died, and as many as 100,000 Iraqis. Afterward, they threw a big parade called the National Victory Celebration. Soldiers and armored troop carriers and flatbed trucks showed off radar communications equipment. An announcer described the planes flying overhead as if it were a pep rally: "One key to air supremacy in the Gulf was the Air Force's F-15 Eagle. . . . Eagles accounted for every Air Force kill during the first ten days of the war." Little boys sitting on their dads' shoulders waved tiny American flags.

I watched with a confusing mixture of pride and guilt and the smug self-assuredness that comes from misplaced moral superiority. *Big men showing off their war machines*, I sneered, thinking about the terrible images I'd seen of Iraqi soldiers burnt to charcoal or bulldozed into giant sand graves, some of them while they were still alive. Like a lot of young, self-righteous liberals who stayed home, I recoiled at the disparities between Iraqi and American dead. Not because I wanted more Americans to die, of course, but because our overwhelming military advantage felt like space-age barbarism. The celebration that followed smacked of chest-thumping. An end zone dance on freshly dug graves.

Sixteen years before, we'd staggered out of Vietnam. Mine was the first generation that grew up in the shadow of a defeated America. I don't know if Vietnam had a direct effect on the way American boys viewed themselves, but it's interesting to look at the kinds of male TV and movie stars that popped up in this era:

Dustin Hoffman, Elliott Gould, Alan Alda. These were different kinds of men from the matinee idols of old. They had less swagger, more sensitivity. Even the sex symbol Warren Beatty had a gentleness about him, more in line with John Lennon than John Wayne.

Was this the new American man? And was this a new kind of America? Not so much.

In the early '80s, the culture swung back toward traditional masculinity with the election of a movie star from an earlier era, Ronald Reagan: tough-talking, cowboy-boot wearing, impenetrable. White House press secretary Marlin Fitzwater once said about his boss, "It's a special enigma of Ronald Reagan, that people who were closest to him still would have trouble telling you what makes him tick." For a large percentage of Americans sick of Woodstock-era navel-gazing, the election of a former Western star as national sheriff probably seemed like a pretty good idea.

It's interesting to compare two movies that came along at this time. *First Blood*, released in 1982 (based on the book from 1972), is about a troubled drifter, a Vietnam veteran who gets caught up in a violent confrontation with a small-town police force. It could easily be seen as an indictment against the kind of aggression its protagonist feels forced into using. Its sequel, *Rambo: First Blood Part II*, came out in 1985 during the height of the "Reagan Revolution." *Rambo* has its protagonist, now fully jacked up, taking up arms on a mission from the U.S. government to find POWs still being held by the Vietnamese ten years after the war's end. Rambo's salvation rests on whether he can redeem the honor of his nation.

The two movies, featuring the same main character only three years apart, demonstrate a profound cultural shift. They're both action films, but their attitudes regarding war feel markedly different. In the first, the hero is scarred by war, reflective, almost sensitive. The country he fought for is literally attacking him; he does not want to fight, resorting to violence only when every other option has failed. It's a constrained, humble look at the pain men face in the service of their nation. In the second, the government gives Rambo a chance at redemption by returning to the country in which he once fought.

In the opening scene, Rambo asks his commanding officer, "Sir, do we get to win this time?"

"This time," the officer says, "it's up to you."

One man, the right man, can refight the entire Vietnam War all by himself. The violence now is triumphal, cartoonish, a dick-wagging macho revenge fantasy. The movie's message echoed the message of Reaganism: America is back.

And for a while, for some Americans, it felt good to be back. The Berlin Wall came down, the Soviet Union fell. Liberalism seemed to be on the rise everywhere. That's the world you were born into, a world of unrivaled American dominance. People were fat and happy and making a lot of money. I got hired to play a sock puppet for TV commercials advertising a new way to buy dog food over the Internet. Mom and I bought our first house. We had a baby. It was 2001.

Seven months later, you were in your bouncy chair watching morning TV with me as the second plane hit the World Trade Center. Even then you loved watching TV, a blessing because the last thing Mom and I wanted to do first thing in the morning was actually parent.

One of the great things about seven-month-olds is that they are not particular about what they watch on TV. We'd gotten into the habit, you and I, of starting our day together with the news. When we turned it on that morning, the first plane had already hit. The early reports were all over the place. Local anchors relayed confused and conflicting information about what had just happened: Was it a small plane? A big plane? As they talked, they showed an image of the smoking building and I remember watching a small dot disappear behind the buildings, another plane. I don't know why, but my eye fixated on the distant dot, and I remember thinking that it hadn't reappeared on the other side of the buildings the way it should have. No part of me thought it was going to slam into the second World Trade Center building. No part of me believed that eighteen years later, we'd still be accounting for that morning. No part of me worried, in that moment, about sending my son to war.

I remember how happy you were in your little chair, scooping fistfuls of Cheerios into your mouth. Bounce, bounce, bounce. I ran upstairs to wake up Mom.

Another plane crashed into the Pentagon. Another into a Pennsylvania field. We watched the Twin Towers fall. The skies went quiet after that.

You were born into a world of American peace, but have grown up in a world of American war. Now you're at an age when boys like you are joining that war. They volunteer for all the reasons boys—and now girls—go to war. Honor, adventure, purpose, patriotism, money for college. You will almost certainly never serve because we are relatively wealthy, and the wealthy do not fight this nation's wars. They do internships at software companies. They do gap years. Scoop ice cream for spending money.

When I watched the First Gulf War unfold on TV, I could not foresee that I would one day have my own son, a daydreamer who has never raised a fist in anger (although you did crack the television screen with your Nintendo Switch controller once after getting pissed off at a videogame). I cannot bring myself to imagine you, even for an instant, in the terror of war. I know your heart too well. But I've known other parents who have waved goodbye to their own daydreaming sons, boys with hearts just the same as yours. Are those boys any less loving than you? Why should they go while you stay behind?

I asked you if you've ever given thought to military service.

"No," you answered dismissively, as if I'd asked whether you'd like a punch in the nose.

It's the answer I would have given at your age, too, and it's the answer I would probably still give now. But I'm less convinced in my answer.

I remember hanging out with a bunch of combat vets once at a bar in New York. These were young guys, veterans of Afghanistan and the Second Persian Gulf War. One of them had lost a leg in combat. At one point in the evening, he took off his prosthetic leg and instructed everybody to drink beer from it. I took a swig of warm beer from his leg and received congratulatory pats on the shoulder from men who had no business congratulating me for anything.

Over the years, I've met a lot of combat vets my age and younger. I like them. They're generally thoughtful, reflective. But some of them are angry, and some of them adrift. When I've hung out with them, it's immediately apparent that they belong to a world I can never enter. They are generous spirits, but their generosity extends only so far. I have found they welcome me right up to its borders but I can never get inside. They're citizens of another country.

There's a book called *What It Is Like to Go to War* by a reporter and Vietnam veteran named Karl Marlantes. He describes war's horror, but also the "deep savage joy in destruction." He also talks about how "warriors, above all, must fundamentally be spiritual people." If I understand his meaning correctly, he is differentiating between warriors and killers. The killer destroys without compunction. The warrior understands his power enough to mitigate its use and to understand its profound consequences. It's the difference between the first Rambo and the second. The combat vets I've known are much more like the first.

The hours and days that followed that September morning when we watched the little dot disappear in the second tower were horrendous and brutal and sad. But they were also compelling and unifying. I'd never experienced that kind of national unity before, that kind of collective, national outrage, and the nearly unanimous call for vengeance. It felt, perversely, awesome. I mean "awesome" in the literal sense of the word: of being swept up in something enormous beyond the control of any one person. It's *that* feeling I think Marlantes is trying to capture in his book, a primal, male appreciation for the inherent wonderment of power, and the ability to bring that power to bear against our enemies. What does it mean to have that power at your disposal? Marlantes says it feels "godlike."

I would be lying if I said part of me does not want to know what that's like. This dueling instinct to create and destroy feels like an essential component of being male. Or, at least, it feels like an essential component of how *I* understand being male. How many young men have wanted to blow stuff up and to come out on the other side, have dreamed of this "godlike" feeling as they marched off to fulfill what they believe to be their manly destiny? Goldstein quotes Mussolini: "War is to man what maternity is to women."

How much of who we are as men is rooted in our

need to make war and how much of our need to make war is rooted in the way we make men? *War and Gender* devotes 500 pages to that very question. Goldstein's conclusion is that the way we raise men and the way we go to war are two mutually reinforcing systems, endless feedback loops.

We raise boys to go to war; we go to war because of the way we raise boys.

You finally filled out the Selective Service form a couple days ago and mailed it off. It's nothing. A postcard. A transaction. I don't think you will ever be called to serve; there hasn't been a draft in forty-five years and I do not think there will be another. We are still making war, but technology allows us to do so with fewer bodies. Your card will most likely be digitized and stored in some electronic file cabinet somewhere, forgotten.

As a boy, did you lie in bed and dream of your own bravery as I did? Did you think, as I did, that you could be counted on in times of conflict? What does each of us owe our nation? I do not think the answer is nothing; I do not think the answer is everything. I don't know what we owe, but I know that I would happily surrender myself to my country before I surrendered you or your sister. Probably every parent feels the same and yet, generation after generation, it sends its boys to war. Would I do the same? I don't know. I would hate myself for sending you and hate myself for keeping you home. I might grow to hate my country for asking. But it wouldn't be my choice, would it? It would be yours. You would be the one choosing to step onto that airplane taking you God knows where to fight a war not of your making.

What promises and lies did those boys at Gettysburg make to their loved ones before they left home? What promises and lies did they tell themselves? You can wander that battlefield today, as I did when I was a kid, looking for some evidence of those three blood-soaked days. There are thousands of old battlefields just like it all over the world. Places where men have fallen— at different times, in the service of different kings and causes, mostly forgotten now. The men are mostly forgotten, too, as we all will be.

The wars we fight come in many forms, although most do not risk the loss of life and limb. Mostly we fight these battles alone, and they will be no less real to us than the ones to which we attach noble names. There are as many ways to be brave as there are things to fear. I have no idea where your own bravery will inspire you to march. Walk into it the best that you can. Trust yourself. Support the people around you. In the end, I think bravery is just being strong for others when you doubt you can be strong for yourself. The more fiercely you love, the braver you will have to be.

◆◆◆◆

Smoke Signals

Violence Is (Almost) Never the Answer

EVERY NOW AND again, Mom will hear a noise in the middle of the night.

"I heard something downstairs," she'll say, waking me.

I strain my ears to listen.

"Did you hear it?"

"No," I'll say. I never hear it, but then again, my hearing is ruined from my high school punk rock band, and I know that my ears are not a reliable indicator of anything. I already dread the question I know is coming.

"Will you go downstairs and check?"

Oh, God. I really don't want to go downstairs because it's the middle of the night and I'm comfortable and, most importantly, because even though I didn't hear anything, I'm suddenly terrified. What if, this time, somebody actually is in the house? Why is she sending me downstairs to confront my murderer? What I want to say is, "*You* go downstairs," but I can't say that because it would violate the ancient contract between man and woman, the one that says men will be the first to face danger. And because it would be such a dick move.

So then I have to get out of bed and creep downstairs and wander around in the dark praying that nobody's there. Left unanswered is the question of what I'm supposed to do if I should come face-to-face with an intruder. In theory, I guess I'm supposed to kick his ass. In practice, we would most likely have a very awkward conversation.

"Excuse me."

"Oh, hey."

"So . . . are you robbing us or what?"

"Yeah. Would you mind giving me a hand with the flat screen?"

And I would help him. What else could I do? The

options are violence or nonviolence. In that situation, I would much rather take the nonviolent route. On the other hand, if the situation should turn more menacing, I would be forced to defend myself and my family to the best of my limited (nonexistent) abilities.

Ultimately, when Mom sends me downstairs, she's relying on my willingness to use violence if the need should arise even though I am ill-equipped to do so. When things go bump in the night, my only real utility is having the honor of being the first one killed. Which seems unfair. I ask her about it.

"You'd be killed, yeah," Mom says, "but that's your job."

"Getting killed is my job?"

"Yeah. You're the strongest person in the house, so you should go downstairs. That's just common sense."

At this point, *you're* the strongest person in the house. I ask Mom if we should start sending you downstairs in the middle of the night instead of me, but that suggestion doesn't go over well.

Look, I'm certainly willing to do whatever I can to protect all of you, but if it's true that I should learn the craft of violence to do so, it follows that all men should do the same, and then we are back where we started, with men being trained for general mayhem because any one of us may decide, at any moment, to start throwing barstools around. This is the paradox of modern manhood: the culture simultaneously demands men's "civilization" while asking us to retain our capacity for manly violence at the squeak of a floorboard.

We despise violence and revere it. Of course, we are a (cough) civilized society, a society in which violence—except in times of war—is officially condemned but unofficially celebrated. Even today, violence sometimes carries a certain nobility. Watch any video of a neo-Nazi getting punched in the face and you'll see what I mean. People love it. Hell, I love it.

Violence is, and always has been, one of our chief forms of entertainment. We pay eighty bucks through pay-per-view to watch UFC guys wallop each other into literal submission. The biggest movies are about (mostly male) superheroes throwing planetary haymakers at the galaxy's evildoers, then dusting themselves off and having a good laugh about it. You, my son, have person-ally spent a good deal of your childhood playing Super Smash Bros., a videogame about otherwise friendly Nintendo characters dropkicking each other into another dimension.

When you guys were kids, Mom and I struggled a lot about how to limit your exposure to violence. We did our best to police your media consumption; for-bade you from playing violent videogames, especially first-person shooter games; and installed a "kid-friendly" Internet browser on the computer, which was supposed to filter out words like "boobs" and prevent you from seeing anything more traumatizing than what you might find on *America's Funniest Home Videos*. Then you went to a friend's house and watched his favorite movie, an ultraviolent revenge thriller called *Max Payne*, so basically what I'm saying is it was impossible.

When women talk about "guy stuff," they often mean exactly this sort of violent entertainment. Whether it's sports or movies or videogames, it's understood that guys thrill to violence. Some women obviously do, too, but the majority of the audience for this stuff has always been male.

Why? What do we get out of it?

Several studies have shown that animals are similarly drawn to violence. One study, from Vanderbilt University, concludes that violence in mice activates the same "reward pathways" in the brain as sex. Mice pick fights with each other for no other reason than they just want to rumble. Aggression appears to be a primal need in mammals.

But that doesn't exactly explain why people want to watch *other* people inflict violence. If violence triggers the same brain regions as sex, then maybe, as with watching porn, it literally turns us on.

As boys, we grow up understanding that, at some point, we will almost certainly have to confront violence. Whether it's wrestling or play fighting or actual punches being thrown in the parking lot after school, boys know that violence, in some form, will play a part in our childhood. It did in mine. Once, a boy I knew pulled a switchblade on me and called me a kike. Once a high school classmate jumped me in the hallway because I wouldn't let a joke go. In camp, a bigger kid told me I was on his "hit list" and that he would be coming for me in the night. He never did, but I didn't sleep the rest of the week. Once, as a young adult on a New York City street, I got coldcocked in the face because I stepped between a tourist with limited English skills and the three-card monte dealer who was trying to rip him off. I haven't had many fights in my life, but I've had some, and I don't think it will shock you to learn I lost them all.

Those incidents startled me, scared me, hurt me. After I got punched in the face, I couldn't fully close my mouth for two weeks. Violence, and the threat of violence, deflates you. Not, I think, because it causes physical pain but because it steals part of your soul. Worse than the times I received violence, though, are the times I inflicted it. Three times from my childhood trouble me to this day.

The first was when I was about five. My brother had just come from home from the hospital after a surgery to correct his cleft palate. His mouth was swollen and tender; he had stitches in his lip. He must have been in pain. Your uncle and I rarely argued, even as kids, but for whatever reason we got into it that day, and before I knew it, I'd punched him as hard as I could in the mouth, exactly where he'd just had surgery. I remember how satisfying it was to hit him, and how that satisfaction immediately turned to horror when he recoiled from the punch, howling.

The second time was when I was maybe nine. My dad and Beth had just bought their first house together. It was in a new development in an old cornfield torn up for spec houses. All that upturned soil had left rocks everywhere. Right after they moved in, Uncle Eric and I were visiting, wandering the new neighborhood sidewalks, when we ran into a group of kids around our age on the other side of the street, maybe three or four of them. I don't know why, but we started taunting each other. Insults flew back and forth across the road. Before I knew what I was doing, I'd bent down and reached for one of the ubiquitous rocks, grabbed one, and threw it as hard as I could at one of the kids. It hit him square in the head. I can't remember if he fell or not. Eric and I ran away. Later, the boy's father came to my dad's door with his son. Thankfully, he was okay, but they wanted an apology. They got one.

The third time was the worst, unforgivably bad, even though the actual level of violence was the smallest. Because your aunt Susan has Down syndrome, she's always needed somebody to keep a careful eye on her. When we were kids, that duty fell to us boys. I was probably ten years old or so, and we were on summer vacation. Susan and I were the only ones home, so I was on Susan duty for a couple hours. The only adult nearby was Elaine, who was coaching her son's Little League team at a field about a five-minute walk from our house. It felt unfair that I had to sit there on a gorgeous summer day and babysit my sister. Little League practice seemed to be going on forever and I was eager to go out and play. I waited for what felt like hours. I grew angrier and angrier. Why did I have to watch my stupid sister when everybody else got to play outside? I just wanted Elaine to get home so I could be released, but there was no sign of her. Finally, out of frustration, I slapped Susan in the face. I remember it so well. We were sitting together on our brown carpeted stairway, the house was still, and I slapped her. She looked so puzzled. I wanted her to cry. It took a couple slaps. Once the tears came, I left her alone in the house and walked to the ball field to tell Elaine that Susan was crying for some reason, wouldn't stop, and that she needed to come home. It's the worst thing I've ever done.

I've never told anybody about that. Not Mom or my brother or the occasional therapists I've visited over the years. I'm telling you now because I want you to know I'm not holding myself apart from the worst impulses of other men. I have them, too. And, somewhere inside of you, so do you.

When the #MeToo Movement started, a famous line began circulating: "Men are afraid women will laugh at them. Women are afraid men will kill them." I was just a boy when I slapped my sister, but in that moment, I was one of those frightening men.

One of the unspoken truths about being a man is that fear of men isn't confined to women; men are *also* afraid that men will kill them. Everybody is afraid of men for the simple reason that men commit the overwhelming majority of violence. One half of our species does a lot of hurting and killing and one half does not. Why? Why are men so much more prone to violence than women?

As I said, a lot of it is cultural, but part of it is almost certainly biological. The males of most species are more violent than the females. The similarities are especially striking in our closest relative, the chimpanzee. An article in *Nautilus* by Steve Stewart-Williams explains:

> Among humans, males commit around 95 percent of homicides, and are around 79 percent of homicide victims. Among chimps, on the other hand, males commit around 92 percent of "chimpicides," and are around 73 percent of chimpicide victims. In short, the sex difference in lethal aggression in the two species is remarkably similar in size.

On average, men are more aggressive than women. The same hormone that makes us so also makes us, on average, bigger and stronger than our female counterparts. That size discrepancy gives us a physical advantage over women. To offset our advantage, evolutionary biologists believe that women developed a more nuanced set of social skills to deal with men, such as negotiation, cooperation, and persuasion. How else would Mom convince me to go downstairs in the middle of the night to get murdered?

Male violence, whether justified or not, is most often rooted in fear. Think of the types of fear as a pyramid. At the base is the fear of loss of life, your own life or the lives of those under your care. Above that is the fear of scarcity, which is the fear that somebody is going to take your limited amount of stuff, thereby endangering your life or the lives of those under your care; I think most hate-based violence lives in this broad area. At the top of the pyramid are two brother fears: the fear of diminishment in other people's eyes, which is the fear we call "pride," and the fear of letting others down, which is the fear we call "honor." Activating any of these fears may move a man to violence.

Another way of saying this is that traditional masculinity itself is rooted in fear. If Real Men are locked in a perpetual game of *¿Quién es más macho?*, it stands to reason that our fear is a massive vulnerability. How many times have you seen some movie character spit into the dust and mutter something like, "I ain't afraid of nuthin"?

Son, I'm here to tell you, that man is a goddamned liar.

The Real Man can't admit his fears because doing so would leave him emasculated. If he admits to being hurt, then he is vulnerable to further hurt. If he allows his pain to show, he fears his enemies will attack him at his weakest. The Real Man is beset by enemies, always. Always there are others out there threatening to destroy him, to destroy his family, to take everything. It's a bleak way to go through life. Here we men are, supposedly strong, yet not strong enough to tell the truth.

The language of traditional masculinity is an endless series of smoke signals we send up warning the enemy we are not to be trifled with. "Here is a man," we say in the way we drink our coffee (not the more feminine tea). "Here is a man," with the pickup we drive, the clothes we wear, the curt way we nod to each other in the elevator. It's every niggling, exhausting detail of our lives informing all who dare gaze upon us that we are men. Not because we are strong but because we are scared others will think we are weak.

Most men are not going to become violent, but many do. The National Coalition Against Domestic Violence says that 1 in 4 women (and 1 in 7 men) "have been the victim of severe physical violence by an intimate partner in their lifetime." It is not only men that commit domestic violence, but it is most often men. The next time some guy shoots up a mall or a movie theater or a school, you will find that he probably has a history of violence against women. According to *The Washington Post*, of 156 mass shootings between 2009 and 2016, "54% . . . were related to domestic or family violence."

We have heard so many women amplify their voices

on this subject in the last couple years, women who have suffered at the hands of men, been overwhelmed by men, feel exhausted and defeated by men. Not all men, we say, stupidly. But when these women tell their stories, they are almost always about men. To say that men do these things is not to condemn all men, but from the perspective of a survivor, that matters very little. It's you and me. It's men.

My dad's wife Beth used to play an album of Kenny Rogers' greatest hits all the time when we were kids. There's a song on there called "Coward of the County" about a regretful father on his deathbed cautioning his son against the violence that ruined his life and the life of his own father.

Pretty good advice from ol' Kenny. Then again, at the end of the song, the son basically kills a bunch of guys in a bar fight for sexually assaulting his girlfriend. "Sometimes," the son decides, "you gotta fight to be a man."

Here, outside the world of movies and videogames and country songs, you will almost never be in a situation where you *have* to choose violence, but when something goes bump in the night, whether you like it or not, it's still your job to confront the danger. It's what you do as a man for the people you love. Then, when you get to the bottom of the stairs, take a breath, and step into the darkness.

NINE

Winner, Winner, Chicken Dinner

Take Pride, but Not Too Much

I ONCE HAD a conversation with a former NFL player, an enormous man, maybe six and a half feet tall, and even five years into retirement still in tremendous physical shape. As you know, I'm not a big football fan, but I'm fascinated by the intense physicality of the game. I asked him about getting hit. Was there any way to give an approximation to somebody like me who has never experienced that kind of violence? He struggled to put the sensation into words, explaining that sometimes you could prepare for the hit, juke a little the moment before impact to lessen the force, use your own motion to offset the worst of it. But, he said, sometimes you just don't see it coming. Sometimes somebody just knocks the shit out of you.

"What's that like?" I asked.

"It hurts," he said, and we both laughed.

He said there were times when he got hit so hard that he was knocked unconscious for a second or two. When that happened there would be a moment when he didn't know if he could get back up. But, he told me, he did. Every time.

"Didn't you ever just want to leave the field?" I asked.

"Naw," he said.

"Why not? What kept you getting back up?"

He thought about it for a second before answering: "Pride."

Before his desire to win the game or earn his paycheck or anything else, pride. And it was easy to hear that pride in his voice. But I also thought I heard something else—and obviously I'm interpreting here—underneath that pride, I thought I heard just the tiniest bit of bafflement. It was like he knew the answer to a math question, but couldn't explain how he arrived at the solution.

Earlier in the day, I'd been with him, his wife, and some other people. We were talking about summer plans and somebody asked him about a resort where he liked to vacation. He described it but couldn't remember the name. "I forget shit all the time," he said.

"It's not from football," his wife jokingly assured us, but the van we were riding in got quiet for a moment before the rest of us made our own jokes about memories failing with age. I know everybody was thinking the same uncomfortable thoughts about the effects of a long football career on this seemingly perfect physical being in our midst, and I found myself wondering about that baffling word "pride."

Pride can be great. When we achieve a goal, we take pride in our accomplishment. When a family member or close friend does the same, we may experience some reflected glory in their victory. I remember you telling me that you were the 236th best player in the world of a certain level of a videogame. You said it to me in an "isn't this stupid" kind of way because it was such a silly and obscure accomplishment, but I could also tell that you felt a tiny amount of legitimate pride about it. And you know what? I felt proud of you, too. I mean, being 236th best in the world at anything is pretty cool because, hey, there are seven billion people out there. Most of us can't claim to be the best at anything. The competition is so fierce and so unrelenting that when we manage to eke out a victory—or a 236th-place finish—it's no wonder that we feel some measure of pride. On those occasions, I say, "Good on ya, boy."

The problem with pride is how, like strength, it can be so easily misapplied and abused. A lot of guys will do anything to preserve their pride. We'll kill for our pride, and die for it. Our gender is based on measuring ourselves against every other member of our gender. The more we can do to stand out, even a little bit, the better we feel about ourselves, and the more pride we may take in our abilities or our good fortune. Without those prideful moments, we may feel as if we don't matter at all.

I used to play a lot of Scrabble. It's a game where men and women should be equally matched, yet every World Scrabble Champion and runner-up since the competition began in 1991 has been male. In his 2001 book about competitive Scrabble, *Word Freak*, Stefan Fatsis notes, "More women than men play [Scrabble] competitively, yet the top experts are overwhelmingly male."

Men dominate the upper ranks of games in which gender should play no role: chess, backgammon, poker, pool, competitive Monopoly (yes, there is competitive Monopoly). Why do female players lag their male counterparts in these games? "Probably because they have lives outside of this shit," said one male Scrabble competitor when asked this question in the book.

I think that guy's observation is exactly correct. Guys are far more inclined than girls to orient their lives around "this shit"—whatever that shit may be—for the same reason they do everything else. We do it to stake out our place in the world, to move a little farther up on the Infinite Axis of Manliness.

It's why a guy will literally memorize *The Official Scrabble Players Dictionary*, as most of the top (male) Scrabble players have done.

One top-ranked player is Joel Sherman, nicknamed "G.I. Joel" because of his frequent gastrointestinal problems. At the time of the book's writing, he was unmarried, slight, asthmatic, and unemployed. He lived with his elderly father and brother in their childhood home in the Bronx. I think it's fair to say he didn't have much of a life outside of Scrabble. Winning the National Championship title, he said, "validated his existence."

It took winning a board game competition with little money or prestige involved for G.I. Joel to feel like he even mattered in the world. Which is, I'm sorry, a little sad. At the same time, though, how awesome that he even found something that *could* give him that measure of pride.

I actually find myself a little envious of Joel Sherman. After all, I'll never be the best at anything. Most of us won't. I *think* I'm okay with that by this point in my life, but I'm not *sure* that I'm okay with it.

Another game I've spent too much time on is poker. I've devoted thousands of hours of my life to playing and studying the game. In poker, the score is kept with money. The more money you're winning, the better you're doing.

If you add up my winnings over all those thousands of hours, I've probably made close to zero dollars. That's right, zero. I might even be a losing player over my life. So why keep playing? And why are poker rooms everywhere filled with men? (Yes, it's almost all men.)

In a word: pride.

Not because we fool ourselves into believing we are better poker players than we actually are, although most of us do that, too. A friend of mine used to date a professional poker player. At the time, he was one of the best poker players in the world. I asked her once about his attitude toward the game—why had he devoted so much of his life to it? She said she thought he played the game because, on some level, he was trying to set right a disordered universe. It seemed like such a grandiose idea, but the more I thought about it, the more it seemed like she might be on to something. I think that's why a lot of guys play games so intensely—a mistaken belief, stemming from pride (vanity, really), that we have it within our power to control uncontrollable outcomes.

Games are such powerful expressions of traditional

masculinity because they are self-ordering. At the end of a game, you know whether you have won or lost. You know your place. Games create status, however short-lived. When we cannot dominate with our muscles, we dominate with our Scrabble tiles. Or our poker chips. Or an amazing guitar solo. Or a perfectly grilled steak. Anything. Everything.

In the end, of course, that's hubris. No matter how good we get at anything, we cannot control outcomes. In the trailer for the movie *Word Wars*, a movie about competitive Scrabble, one of the competitors says, "In this game, you can beat God if you've got the right tiles."

Leave it to a dude to try to beat God.

Which brings me to another rule of traditional masculinity: win. A Real Man wins. He wins and wins and when he is done winning, he wins some more. "You will get tired of all the winning," our president promised when he ran for office. When he disagrees with somebody, his go-to insult is "loser." In the minds of certain men, there is no greater shame than loss.

Which is too bad because we are all doomed to failure. All people fail as much as, or more than, we succeed. That's a good thing. We learn more from our losses than from our victories. Loss sets us back and propels us forward. But if our pride doesn't allow us to accept failure, we get stuck. We get defensive. We get angry and arrogant. That's why it's so hard for some guys to say, "I'm sorry."

A better rule than "win": approach your tasks with humility, not pride. Your life will be filled with wins and losses however you define those terms, and you will be immeasurably happier if you can accept both with grace.

To be fair, you're actually pretty good about accepting defeat and about apologizing. It's your sister who has a hard time with both. If something goes wrong, the fault never lies with her. You're the opposite: you always put the blame on your own shoulders. They're both kind of the same thing, strategies for dealing with wounded pride. One person takes no responsibility; one person takes too much. Mom is more like Ruthie, and I'm a lot more like you. I've always been like that. When my brother and I were kids, we got into a fight about something and he kept trying to blame me for whatever had gone wrong. Finally, out of frustration, I yelled back him, "Fine! It's my fault! No matter what happens forever it will always be my fault!" And, all these years later, somehow it is.

I'm kidding. Kind of.

I THINK A lot of guys get into trouble when we confuse "pride" with "dignity." Don't fall into that trap. "Pride" and "dignity" are not interchangeable. "Pride" is something that comes from accomplishment or association. "Dignity" is inherent. It's a birthright. Pride is something that distinguishes one person from another. Dignity is the glue between us. We all have, or should have, a fundamental sense of dignity, the sense that we matter not because of what we've done but because we simply are. You matter. The things you do matter, too, but who you are matters more. That's your dignity.

That same president who disparages other people as losers operates solely from a place of pride. Whatever dignity he may have once had is no longer apparent. One of the dangers of demagogues, though, is their expertise at manipulating *your* pride. Think about the slogan "Make America Great Again," which has been used to twist national pride against itself by diminishing everything and everybody that doesn't match the narrow definition of "America" that its advocates are trying to make "great again." Or think about the terms "black pride" and "white pride," which have nearly opposite meanings. "Black pride" is a term used to acknowledge and affirm dignity, whereas "white pride" describes a trait in those who tear down the dignity of others.

I suspect men in particular are vulnerable to this kind of manipulation because it conjures the language of traditional masculinity. If you are "losing," it's because somebody else is "winning," most likely somebody undeserving or nefarious. Most men are willing to take our losses, but only if we believe the game is fair. When somebody comes along and tells us that the rules are rigged, that some people are given special treatment or an unfair advantage, we may respond to that message because it validates the common nagging suspicion that the reason we feel ourselves losing is because, at bottom, we're losers. Don't fall for it.

Dignity allows for humility. If you believe in your

own self-worth, it costs you nothing to admit fault, or to turn the other cheek when insulted. Your dignity does not need to defend itself.

Respectful pride can enhance your dignity and lift up the people around you. Taking pride in yourself, your surroundings, and your community can, and should, serve as motivation for yourself and others. By all means, take pride in who you are and the things you have done. After all, you're the 236th best player of one level of *Donkey Kong Country: Tropical Freeze.*

Sometimes I worry that you're unwilling to put enough of yourself forward to risk failure. When Mom and I got on you about schoolwork, that was the most frustrating thing to me. Not that you might get a bad grade, but that you wouldn't risk enough of yourself to try to get a good grade. What if you studied hard and failed? What if you worked your ass off on an essay and it kind of sucked? What if you tried as hard as you could and still came up short? It's one thing to skate through school with so-so grades knowing that you could have done better; it's another to go through school with so-so grades knowing that you could not.

One of the most humbling things about being a parent is feeling powerless to prevent your kid from making the same mistakes you did. We've talked about how I was a middling student and how much I regret it now. Not because I care about grades, but because I know that my bad habits in school ended up becoming bad habits I still have as an adult. Like you, I too often skate by because I can. Even when I try to fight it, I end up falling back into old patterns, patterns of procrastination and generalized blowing-shit-off that I hate about myself and worry that I see in you. And I worry that we do it for the same reason: What if you try so hard to win but still end up losing? What if you give everything you have to something and it still isn't enough? What if, in loss, you conclude that *you* are not enough?

You are enough.

I tell it to you and I believe it for you, just as I believe it for everybody. We are given all the gifts we need to make our way through this world. You have a good brain and a healthy body and, on occasion, you even remember to chew with your mouth closed. Unlike many, you also have some extra gifts: your education, background, and relative financial comfort. Your challenge will be to believe in yourself enough to fail, to learn to take pride in the effort instead of the outcome.

As you leave, I want you to find ways to take pride in the small things you do. The little daily stuff. Washing a dish. Folding your laundry. Whatever. It's a mindfulness practice, a way of giving your attention and care to something that nobody will notice but you. You can't "win" at folding a shirt, but you can do it well. I hope you find pride in what you do, who you love, and who you are. Allow your pride to stand you up. Don't let pride stand in your way.

TEN

♦♦♦♦

Gunslinger

You Can't Do It Alone

Now that you're eighteen, it drives you crazy when somebody tells you what to do or how to do it. When you went to prom this year, I remember the look of resignation on your face as Mom helped you fit the black tuxedo studs into your buttonholes for you. I laughed because you obviously wanted her to buzz off so you could do it yourself, but at the same time, I don't think you had any idea what you were supposed to do with them. So you grimaced and endured your mother dressing you for what will probably be the last time in your life. I also know you never would have asked for help. Instead you would have gone to prom with your tuxedo shirt buttoned with regular buttons like a god-damned peasant.

It's been kind of funny seeing how your independence has asserted itself over time, because you're a man under the law, but a man who still has to be taught how to use a credit card, put gas in the car, fill out a financial aid form. Because of pride, you don't want to be told how to do anything, yet you have no idea how to do nearly any of the mundane tasks of adulthood.

Every child eventually craves independence, and despite all those nagging moms and dads reminding their kids to use the bathroom before getting in the car, every parent wants their kid to become independent, too. From a parent's point of view, we're looking for reassuring clues that our children will be able to take care of themselves when they leave home. From a kid's point of view, parents are annoying.

I think independence has a special resonance with boys because traditional American masculinity leaves us highly susceptible to the idea of the "self-made man," he who lifts himself up through toil and talent without the appearance of any assistance at all. He's Benjamin Franklin, Thomas Edison, Steve Jobs. He's David Blaine levitating from a sidewalk. As with all magic tricks, the "self-made man" is an illusion.

It's worth a quick historical detour to talk about the origins of the phrase "self-made man." Kentucky senator Henry Clay is widely credited with first using the term during a speech in 1832 in which he defined self-made men as those "who have acquired whatever wealth they possess by patient and diligent labor." It's a definition with which most of us would probably still agree. What's interesting about Clay's speech, though, is its context: a defense of American manufacturing against foreign corporations. The "enterprising and self-made men" to whom he refers are Southern factory owners who, he argues, can compete with the more technologically advanced factories of Great Britain because of two factors: "water-power and labor." The labor is slave labor. Those budding Kentucky industrialists, men who have acquired wealth through patient and diligent labor, are, in fact, utterly dependent on the sweat of the enslaved.

Despite this inherent contradiction, the phrase gained popularity over the coming decades, and came to represent an American ideal enveloped in our founding credo: independence. The American experiment contained the promise of self-creation. It's a romantic idea, one that has animated the American spirit for centuries.

The history we teach ourselves is one of rugged individualists blazing new paths, often literally. They are frontiersmen, cowboys, astronauts. Out there—on the dusty Western mesas, on the vast and tumbling sea, or in the endless maw of outer space—every moment is a battle against forces greater than oneself. The Real Man will tame the savage things and make them his own. He is rough and he is ready, and when you break down the idea of the self-made man even for a second, you realize it's all bullshit.

I really mean that—it's such pernicious, colossal bullshit. For starters, patriarchal societies have always kept women more tightly bound to men than men to women, making true independence for one half of our species almost impossible. And the whole notion is harmful because it creates a false narrative about who we men are in society, what we do, and who we owe. Nobody goes it alone now, and they never did. The first European colonizers arrived by the shipload with the backing of corporate sponsors and vast militaries, then relied on the Native population to survive. As the nation matured and pushed westward, the famous American frontiersmen went forth under the protection of a new government handing out land like Halloween candy to anybody who wanted it (so long as the people who wanted it were white men). Wagon trains of pioneers set forth, using the safety of numbers—and the safety provided by scattered military outposts—to cross the country.

Is it even possible to go it alone? Is there any of us who, through some alchemical mixture of fortitude, cunning, and luck, forms himself, like Adam, from the dust? Even the American who might have the greatest claim to such a story says no. In 1859, Frederick Douglass gave a speech entitled "Self-Made Men," in which he said:

"We have all either begged, borrowed or stolen. We have reaped where others have sown, and that which others have strown, we have gathered. It must in truth be said, though it may not accord well with self-conscious individuality and self-conceit, that no possible native force of character, and no depth or wealth of originality, can lift a man into absolute independence of his fellowmen, and no generation of men can be independent of the preceding generation."

We are who we are because of those who surround us, and those who came before. Our lives are made possible because of the unknown number of people upon whom we lean. We call those people "society." Any society is just an agreement between people to help each other out. An individual within that larger group may do great things, but it is the larger collective body that supports them. When we take pride in the accomplishments of our neighbors or countrymen, it's because we have some stake, however small, in their success. None of us travels as far as we might without walking at least some of the road others have laid.

The choices you make will be your choices. I think we've given you a good foundation to make something of yourself, but just know that though fortune may favor the bold, it prefers the privileged.

Time and again, we see that the people most likely to succeed are the people with the most resources at their disposal to help them achieve their goals. They have some combination of stable home lives, good schools, mentors, community support, access to finances. Yes, there will always be people who overcome terrible adversity. Those people deserve to be celebrated, but you shouldn't have to be extraordinary to be successful.

Think about all the people for whom terrible adversity ends up being overwhelming. Were they born with any less promise than you? Do they deserve any less success?

Boys no less smart or talented than you begin their lives in terrible circumstances—maybe poverty, addiction, neglect—and cannot ever find their way free.

Are those boys self-made, too? Or do we acknowledge that circumstances contribute to the lives we end up living?

The myth of the self-made man tells us he owes nothing to others for his place in the world. Yet all of us accrue debt, good and bad. Some of it is payment owed to those who helped us along the way. Some of it is reparations due to those we harmed. I don't know if it's possible to ever make good on what we owe, but I know those debts are real, and they will suffocate you if you don't make some effort to pay them down. Those debts are a good thing because they tether us to one another. Ignoring them leaves us defiant, proud, and alone.

It's funny how acknowledging the simple truth of what we owe to one another threatens to upend traditional masculinity. All debt leaves us vulnerable, but rather than view our debts as a liability, I would argue that debt can be a source of strength and motivation for the erstwhile self-made man. Without those debts, you end up like some bloodless Ayn Rand character, indifferent to others because you can only see their flawed humanity as an impediment to your own achievements. (If you don't know who Ayn Rand is, you'll probably find out in college because it seems like every boy devours her books *Atlas Shrugged* and *The Fountainhead* when they are looking for an excuse to be an asshole. I know I did.)

The best way we pay off the people we owe is to live good and productive lives. It's what I expect of you and your sister. The things that you make—family, creative projects, money—those will be *your* things. You will be able to say, and should say, that your triumphs are yours, but they aren't yours alone.

The best illusions convince us of one thing when the reality is something else. So it is with the self-made man. A constrained masculinity asks us to embrace this illusion because it venerates independence to the exclusion of our shared interdependence, which is viewed as somehow more feminine.

Think about all those movie gunslingers who ride into town to shoot up the baddies. When beleaguered townspeople call upon the services of that lone ranger, they're asking for the rough help of a masculine force to clean up the messes of their soft and feminized culture. After the dust settles, the gunslinger collects his due, gets a handshake from the hapless sheriff and a tearful embrace from the girl whose brother's death he avenged. Then he mounts his faithful steed and trots out of town, alone, toward the endless, lonesome sunset.

He is a man who owes nothing and is owed nothing. When he disappears over the horizon, he is gone for good. Ultimately, that's the promise of the self-made man. He stands alone and he stands apart. And, as I said, he's a fantasy.

I want you to dream big. I want you to do everything in your power to activate your ideas. You might end up taking them very far. I hope you do. I hope you recognize the people who help you along the way and I especially hope that you don't trample on others to get to where you want to go. Instead, gather people close. Allow your successes to be theirs; the sunsets you ride into will be a lot more enjoyable with others at your side.

When I told you I was writing a chapter on self-made men, you smirked and pointed at yourself. Then you made yourself a peanut butter and jelly sandwich with the ingredients I bought for you at the grocery store. I laughed.

ELEVEN

◆◆◆◆

Lucky Charms

Choose Happiness

IT'S MY WEDDING day. I'm alone in a hotel room getting dressed for the ceremony. Your mom and I have a room for a couple nights because we've given your grandparents our place while they're in New York, and we thought it'd be fun to stay someplace special. Mom left hours ago. She's getting ready at our friend Kerri's place downtown, surrounded by her ladies-in-waiting: Kerri, her friend Romy, Grandma Sue, and Kerri's mom Sharon.

I lay my new suit out on the bed. Hugo Boss. The most expensive article of clothing I have ever bought. Still a hell of a lot cheaper than Mom's dress, and at least I'll wear the suit more than once. Dark gray jacket and pants, periwinkle shirt, striped tie. Uncle Eric and my friend David are going to stand for me at the service. They'll meet me at the church later. For now, I'm alone.

I get dressed, re-knotting the tie several times until I get the length right. New black shoes. I walk outside into a gorgeous October New York City afternoon. The church is ten or twelve blocks away. We'd gone back and forth about where we would marry. Church, civil service, temple . . . In the end, Mom's active Catholicism outweighed my unobserved Judaism, and we picked a modern church right across the street from our apartment building. A homeless guy asks me for money. I open my wallet and hand him a twenty-dollar bill.

"Hey, thanks," he says.

"I'm getting married!" I say.

"Great," he says, pocketing the money.

My dad was twenty-two or twenty-three when he met my mom, around the same age I was when I started seeing your mom. They met at Indiana University, as far as I know the first romantic relationship for either of them. Dad was a shy and soft-spoken kid from Queens,

New York. I wish I knew exactly how they met and how their courtship unfolded. They had some superficial similarities: both second-generation Jews, eldest children, city kids. Beyond that, I don't know what they shared other than their own loneliness.

The year before, my mom had suffered something like a nervous breakdown. The circumstances remain a little cloudy, but I think I have a good idea of what happened. In high school, she'd developed a friendship with a couple a few years older than her whose children she babysat for. Unhappy at home, Mom spent a lot of time hanging out at their house with the mom while the husband worked. They became close friends. After graduation, my mom went off to college, returning home every now and again to babysit.

One weekend, the couple went away for a couple days, leaving Mom with two little kids to watch. By itself, a weekend alone with two toddlers might be enough to cause most eighteen-year-olds to have a nervous breakdown. I was nearly thirty when you guys came along and, trust me, you guys almost did me in a few times. Something happened with my mom that weekend, though, that crossed a line. When the couple returned from their weekend trip, something happened—some outburst—that resulted in a call to my mother's parents to pick up their hysterical daughter.

My grandparents came for their daughter and, against her will, put her in a psychiatric hospital for six weeks, where she underwent repeated courses of electroshock therapy. Mom later told me she didn't remember much from this period of her life; the shock therapy erased her memories. I interviewed her several times during the last couple years of her life, and piecing everything together, I think I have a good idea of what caused her breakdown.

Mom had been lonely and unhappy at home, and also lonely at school. She felt most comfortable, most herself, with this couple, and especially with the woman of the couple. That relationship became increasingly important to my mom. When she left them for school, I think she missed her friend, and I think distance deepened her feelings. Over time, away from home for the first time, I think Mom fell in love.

When the couple came home from their weekend

together, my mom said she "caused a scene." She doesn't remember exactly what she said, but I can easily imagine my voluble mother, in an explosive outburst, confessing her love to the woman.

Of course I'm speculating, but whatever she said was significant enough to land her in the hospital. There, the doctors tried to "cure" her homosexuality using the standard method of the day: pumping the brain with thousands of volts of electricity. The only thing the shock therapy accomplished, she told me in our interviews, was that it made her hate her parents.

What was it like for her to return to school the following year? She must have been craving quiet, normalcy. She found it in a shy boy from Queens. I wonder how much she told him about what she'd been through. Maybe some, maybe none at all.

From my dad's perspective, I suspect he just wanted a girlfriend, the way I did when I was his age. The way you do right now. Somehow, they became a couple. I like to think of them in the beginning of their relationship being sweet to each other, and kind. Talking. I hope that's what it was like. I hope they were friends.

Within a year, they married. In their wedding photos, they look young and heartbreakingly hopeful.

My parents' marriage lasted almost nine years, from 1968 to 1976. In that time, they had three kids, bouncing from Chicago to Washington State, back to Chicago, and, finally, to New Jersey. By the time they began divorce proceedings, so much had changed. The Vietnam War had ended, the sexual revolution had begun. Women were marching for equality. And my mom had fallen in love with the lady down the street. This time, her feelings were reciprocated. If my parents' marriage had been a symptom of the old order, their divorce was a result of the new. New gender roles, new sexual expression, new opportunities. But also a new anger among those who preferred things the way they'd been. A cultural backlash that we're still feeling today.

To his credit, my dad never expressed anger to us kids at the way his marriage had panned out. He never badmouthed my mom, never said anything homophobic or mean-spirited about her relationship with Elaine.

When he left, my dad took a little apartment near our house. We kids would head over there every other weekend to hang out, get McDonald's, run around the shabby playground across the street. On Sunday nights, he'd drop us off and we'd run up the sidewalk to our house while he stayed in the car. We could see his headlights backing out through the slats in the living room vertical blinds.

I wish I could ask him now about those days. What was it like for him to come home to that empty apartment every night, his life so different from the one he must have imagined when he walked down the temple aisle in his own new suit?

It's weird to me how marriage and fatherhood have become the cornerstones of my own life. Equally weird is how conventional my life turned out, how far removed from the fantasy life I envisioned for myself as a boy and young man. Here I am, writing from the kitchen counter of our home in the wilds of Connecticut. You and your sister have just left for school. The cat is scraping up the last of his breakfast from his bowl. I feel very much at home and at peace.

Maybe it shouldn't feel weird at all. After all, my life is similar to those of millions of men my age. Fathers, husbands, buyers of cat food. It's all so domestic. Growing up, I thought of domesticity as a curse on the male spirit. It meant compromise. Selling out. It meant, I thought, that The System had won, whatever "The System" was. The status quo, I guess, the same vague rules and regulations I felt pressing in on me as a boy, the same pressures that I blamed for my dad's death: If he hadn't had to work so much, if he hadn't had to take those night classes at Rutgers. If he'd been there for us more. If, if, if. The American dream felt rusty to me, a sucker's bet. As a kid, I determined that I wouldn't fall for it.

Yes, I thought, I'd find somebody to love but I wouldn't marry. A happy marriage seemed as chimerical as everything else. Many of my childhood friends' parents were divorced and of the ones whose marriages remained, none seemed particularly happy.

Will you ever marry?

"Probably," you answer, with a shrug.

Even that noncommittal answer shows so much more optimism than I felt at your age. I didn't think I ever would; I didn't think it was worth the risk.

After my dad died, I started paying more attention to the lives of the men around me. We lived in a U-shaped neighborhood of tightly packed townhouses clustered around a courtyard of assigned parking spaces. My bed was pushed against the bedroom window and, every morning, I'd peer out to watch the neighborhood husbands trudging from their houses, dusting the snow off their windshields with their coat sleeves, driving off to work. Around 5:30 or 6:00, they'd return to their parking spaces, trudge back up their sidewalks, disappear into their houses. Weekends were for running errands, schlepping the kids to soccer games, taking trash bags out to the big dumpster at the end of the road.

I'm not sure what I was looking for when I watched those guys coming and going. Some sign that the life toward which I was heading, the life of a man, was worthwhile. What did "worthwhile" mean, exactly? I couldn't have told you. But I had a sense.

The one thing I knew about my future life as a man was that I wanted to be happy. Maybe that's a dumb thing to say since everybody wants to be happy. But, as I said earlier, nobody ever talked about happiness as a goal, if they talked about it at all. Happiness felt like an accident, an emotional blip you experienced at birthday parties and on the first day of summer vacation. They asked, "What do you want to be when you grow up?" not "What do you think will make you happy when you grow up?"

What's the point of growing up if it's going to suck? Childhood already felt kind of sucky. I wasn't going to let adulthood be the same. Manhood was supposed to be a time of maximal freedom and opportunity, to do all the shit I couldn't do as a kid. Stay out late, travel the world, eat bowls of Lucky Charms all day, every day.

The things that I thought might bring me happiness as an adult seemed incompatible with the lives I saw from my bedroom window. As I've said, boys aren't groomed for happiness. Instead, we're directed toward accomplishment over contentment, every milestone pointing to the next. In some ways, we're conditioned *against* happiness because a happy man could easily become a complacent man. Get enough complacent men together sitting around enjoying themselves and the next thing you know, they're not producing as many goods and services as they might. Then what? The whole whirling machine flies off its gears. Too many people make too much money from other people's unhappiness. Men aren't taught to be happy. We're taught to produce.

The pressure on girls is almost the opposite; their happiness is presumed if (and only if) they fulfill a couple of requirements, all of which are based around the very idea of domesticity. Yes, we now encourage women to have careers, but we don't expect those careers to "fulfill" them in the same way we do for men. A single woman, employed or not, is still thought to be lacking something. Moreover, a childless woman, no matter what else her life holds, is assumed to be lacking something that a childless man is not. The promise for girls, still, is that they will find happiness in marriage and motherhood. Never mind that a study by a behavioral scientist and expert on happiness, Paul Dolan, determined, "The healthiest and happiest population subgroup are women who never married or had children."

As for me, I didn't know what path I could possibly

take to find happiness. A traditional job, I thought, wouldn't do it. Observations from my own life suggested marriage wouldn't do it, either. Or kids. Or anything, really. The only thing I knew for sure was that I needed to get out of New Jersey. As soon as I could, I would pack my shit and go, and I would just keep going. Maybe I would become an actor, traveling from city to city, poor but free, and, hopefully, happy. Was that a man's life?

It certainly didn't align with the men I saw around me or of any man I'd ever met. The closest analogy I could find for what I wanted were the carnies who operated the rides at the annual firemen's fair. Wasn't there a certain nomadic romance about running the ring-toss game in town after town? Maybe you'd meet a local girl and give her a giant stuffed bear even if she didn't win the game, and you'd share a candy apple and make out in the glow of the Tilt-A-Whirl's flashing lights. I didn't want to run off and join the carnival, but I wanted that feeling.

I wanted what a lot of young men want: adventure, independence, escape. I wanted something I couldn't quite name. I wanted out. It just felt to me like there was something better out there—out in the bigness of America—that a guy could find, something more satisfying than money. Longer lasting. I didn't know what it was. Nobody ever put a name to it.

I remember the day Mom and Elaine dropped me off on my first day at NYU. It's late summer. My new dorm is just across the street from Washington Square Park, spiritual home of the East Coast '60s scene a couple decades before. After we haul my stuff into my room, Mom gives me a big hug, sniffling her goodbyes as they leave. It's the moment I've been dreaming about since I could remember. Out of my little house, my little town, the little lives of the people there. I've just turned seventeen and I am free.

I walk outside. The city is humming: chess hustlers leaning over their tables, scrawny pot sellers whispering their wares under their breath as you pass, new students like me in T-shirts and shorts. To my left is Bleecker Bob's Records and the dark old bohemian coffee shops where you can sit for hours stirring your drink and reading old paperbacks. A few blocks east is Tower Records and the big used clothing stores on Broadway. Keep going into Alphabet City, where punk rockers cluster in small groups on the sidewalk with their mangy dogs trying to scrounge up enough money to go drink at the Pyramid or 7B. Or I can turn around and walk deeper into the Village, maybe get a falafel or rummage through a used book store. Up a few blocks is the scruffy movie theater where they show *The Rocky Horror Picture Show* at midnight. Keep going and you end up in what I think of as "New York, New York," the yawning mass of the city's skyscrapers and office towers and brownstones and Central Park and all the places I will never visit when I am in school. That's the go-go New York, where worker bees push buttons on computer keyboards and move money around the world. Down here in Washington Square Park are the artists and wannabe artists like me. We happy few, we pretentious few. We starry-eyed poseurs. I am enthralled with all of it and I spend several minutes taking in the air and watching the people streaming by. My people. I turn to my right and walk a couple blocks. Caffe Reggio, Cafe Wha?, the corner pizza place. I stop, unsure of where to go, what to do. I don't have a lot of money and no real plan. After a few more minutes, I get bored, walk back to my dorm, and start unpacking my shit.

Do you remember that summer vacation we took once to Spain? On the boardwalk there, we saw a street performer who blew giant, person-sized soap bubbles. We watched him pull a child from the crowd and blow a shimmering, iridescent soap bubble around the child's entire body. That's how all of New York felt to me. Like I was inside something fantastical, but also somehow separated from it.

I had friends and things to do and I was working hard in school. Within a couple years, though, I was just as depressed as I'd ever been. I quit school, as I said, to become a Teenage Mutant Ninja Turtle. I remember calling Mom to tell her I'd gotten this crazy job offer and I wanted to go even though it meant dropping out of school for the semester, fully expecting her to chew my head off for even entertaining such a ridiculous idea. She wanted to know why I wanted to take the job.

"They're going to pay me to travel the country," I told her.

She was uncharacteristically quiet on the other end of the phone. I waited for an explosion that never came.

"Just promise me you'll go back to school."

"I promise," I lied.

A few days later, my friend Ben and I were packing up a brand-new, dark blue Chevy Astro van with our duffel bags and two Ninja Turtle sarcophagi containing our costumes and the heavy Turtle heads crammed with electronics and gears that made the eyes and mouths move. We drove into the New York side of the Lincoln Tunnel and came out in America.

Here's a rule for you, or, rather, a wish: If you ever get the chance, drive the country. See it from the ground, mile marker by mile marker. Plane travel doesn't give you the scale of the place. You need to be on the ground. It's not even that there's so much to *see*, even though there *is* so much to see; it's that you need to live in the experience of our immensity.

Being out there, town by town and city by city, was as close as I ever got to being that carny. "Step right up, folks, see a real live rootin'-tootin' radioactive Turtle." It was the kind of otherworldly weirdness I'd read about in Hunter S. Thompson's pieces for *Rolling Stone*, minus the drugs and alcohol. I didn't do anything like that then, and didn't feel like I needed to. Everything was already strange enough. Doing the weather at local TV stations and dancing for kids in Pizza Hut parking lots. Visiting hospitals, marching in the Macy's Thanksgiving Day Parade, standing on the roof of our van in the middle of a Kansas field singing "The Star-Spangled Banner" at the top of our lungs. All of that, and they were paying me. It was great. I felt free. Stinky, but free.

I lasted four months on the road. Twenty-three thousand miles. By the end, I could barely muster the energy to put that fucking twenty-five-pound Turtle head on my shoulders, the weight of it resting squarely on the bridge of my nose. The suit smelled like BO and baby powder. Ben and I still got along, but four months together will strain any friendship. Ironically, the show was called the Coming Out of Our Shells Tour, but the longer I stayed on the road, the more I found myself retreating into my own shell. I knew I needed to leave. Ben enlisted a friend of his from back home in Tennessee to take my place and they dropped me at the airport. I flew back to New York and got a little apartment. My friends were all in school during the day. I walked around the city and tried to be happy.

A couple years later, my friends and I got our TV show, *The State*. I got a little bit famous. The fun of that faded quickly. The show folded; I sold another show. The fun of that faded. I dated, but the fun of that faded. It began to feel like the only thing that gave me any happiness was novelty. If I just kept looking for the next new thing, I could ride my happiness the way Tarzan rode vines, swinging from thing to thing to thing forever. I had dreamed of being an actor and being free. I was an actor and I was free. So why was I still unhappy?

The freedom I thought I'd wanted had been its own kind of trap, a distraction from getting to know myself. I loved so much of it, but it began dawning on me that I wasn't going to ever feel whole if I continued looking for myself outside of myself. That was around the time I started dating Mom.

At first, our relationship was another novelty. Me and a pretty Minnesota girl, a girl who had grown up, like me, just wanting to get out. Like me, she left as soon as she could. First for college in Minneapolis. Then to Paris. Then to D.C. Finally, she came to New York. Like me, she had an older brother and a younger sister with a mental disability. She was (and is) smart, funny, challenging. After a little while, she moved in. We hung out with friends, walked down to Ben & Jerry's on warm nights. Squabbled. Made up. Ate a lot of buffalo wings. A few years later, I asked her to marry me.

Even when I asked, I didn't know if it was the right thing for me, or for us. We were celebrating Christmas a couple of days early because we were traveling to Minnesota the next day to be with her family. After we'd exchanged presents, I took out the ring. "Will you marry me?" I asked.

"I don't know," she said.

Which seemed about right. Neither of us knew. Would marriage be just another vine to swing on for a moment? Or would it provide something more sustaining for me, and for us?

What changed? Why did I decide to take a chance on marriage when I didn't know if I even believed in it? First, I loved your mom. We'd been together a few years and I didn't see any reason why we would break up. So, my thinking went, if we're not going to break up, maybe we should take the next step. Of course I worried. Of course I knew that marriages often fail, but I thought maybe ours would not. That maybe it would be worth the risk. If it ended, it ended; at least we would have tried.

Then it's eight months later and we're at the altar exchanging our I-do's. We kiss and sign some fancy calligraphed document attesting to our new status as wife and husband. We walk down the aisle, through the big wooden doors, and outside into the sun to receive our congratulations. That was twenty years ago, and this feels like a really awkward time to tell you that Mom and I are getting divorced.

(That's a joke.)

Our reception is at a quirky club in Midtown. In a few years, it will be a carpet store. Our wedding photographer buzzes around. We've got a few of those photos hanging on our bedroom wall. In one of the pictures, I'm at the reception, some friends on either side of me. One of them leans toward me, talking. I'm listening and not listening, there and not there, a little smile on my face. It's my dad's smile.

As you get older, I think you'll discover the way time seems to bend in on itself. One event ties to another and to another and to another. Back and forth. Lives and people and events all wrapped together. One minute you're a boy dreaming of escape, and then you do. You're dreaming of finding love, and then you do. You get married, have a son, then a daughter, and it feels like they're babies for so long, but then your son is leaving for college and you find yourself close to tears in the cereal aisle at the supermarket because they're playing that Harry Chapin song, "Cat's in the Cradle," and you feel like an idiot because you're standing there with a box of Grape-Nuts clutched to your chest thinking about your own dad who never saw you become a father yourself and never knew his grandkids and because all stories about men are, at least in part, stories of fathers and sons, our lives as knotted up together as old ropes.

I'm at the kitchen island drinking my morning tea. I've got stuff to do today, writing and working, taking out the trash, maybe getting the car washed. I'm starting to think about what I'm going to make for dinner tonight. I don't know how many more dinners we'll all have together. Soon you'll be gone and it'll just be the three of us. Then Ruthie will go and it'll just be me and Mom out here in the wilds of Connecticut. I remember getting dressed the day of my wedding and almost feeling like I was being carried along by something. Marriage and chores and family dinners to come. This isn't the life I thought I'd have. I can't tell you for sure if it's better or worse than what I imagined for myself as a kid. What I can tell you is I'm happy.

TWELVE

It's Just Plumbing

*Communicate with Your Partner
(and Pick Up the Check)*

WE MIGHT NEVER have kissed if she hadn't yelled at me. Mom and I were on our first date, a shopping excursion to SoHo. We'd piddled around downtown for a couple hours, then we came back to my little apartment and hung out on my ratty thrift store couch talking . . . and talking . . . and talking. Hours went by. Finally, she told me she was going to leave.

"Okay," I said.

"Unless you want me to stay," she said.

"If you want."

She became exasperated with me. "I just don't know what we're doing here!"

I didn't know, either! That was the problem. It wasn't even clear to me that our date was a date. We hadn't used the word. We'd just agreed to do something together over the Thanksgiving holiday when everybody else was out of town. Was that a date? I'd hoped it was, but I wasn't sure. There was also the small matter of the fact that she was living with her boyfriend at the time.

She'd made it clear to me that she wasn't that into him, but I didn't want to be the guy seducing somebody already involved with somebody else. I didn't know what was going on between us and I didn't want to be presumptuous. What if she didn't want me to kiss her? What if, like so many other girls, she just thought of me as a friend? Maybe she only wanted to hang out and flirt and go home to wait for her boyfriend to return from his family visit.

I didn't know and I was afraid to make the first move. Of course, it would have been simple enough for her to lean over and kiss me. So why didn't she? Because she was as caught up in the same gender hang-ups as me. Kissing me first would have violated her own archaic sense of sex roles. Instead, we talked and talked and nobody was kissing anybody.

Finally—after she yelled at me—I got the message. I stood up and kissed her.

I'd been struggling with questions about what we now call "consent" for years before this moment. Not because I overstepped, but because I tended to under-step, which is to say I was so worried about offending somebody that I missed social cues that perhaps would have been obvious to most other people.

I'm writing to you about relationships with women because you've told me you like girls, but anything I say here would apply to any kind of relationship. When I was eighteen, I spent a summer as an intern at the Williamstown Theatre Festival. I heard a story there about a very famous (and famously married) actor who hit on another, younger actor. When the younger actor said he wasn't gay, the older actor replied, "It's just plumbing, my boy." Whatever I say in this chapter applies to everybody, regardless of plumbing.

Growing up in a lesbian and feminist household, I'd

been raised to believe that men and women are equal, and that (to paraphrase Orwell) women are slightly more equal than men. This created some awkward moments when I started dating because I was so nervous about appearing sexist that I refused to pay for my date's dinners, insisting that we go dutch. My reasoning was simple: I didn't want my dates to think that I expected anything from them in return for dinner and a movie; I was trying to protect my dates from, I guess, me. In retrospect, I'm mortified at my own doofy behavior. Nothing kills a romantic vibe more than trying to figure out how much she owes for the calamari.

I was still doing this when I first began dating Mom. Thankfully, she endured my early dating faux pas with grace and has only made merciless fun of me about it for the last twenty years.

Here's some advice from father to son: don't split the bill with your date. If you ask her out, you should pay. That's not sexist—it's the polite thing to do. If she asks *you* out, you might also volunteer to pay because that's also polite, but hopefully she insists and then you have a little pretend argument about it, which hopefully ends with one of you saying to the other something like, "Was this our first fight?" and then laughing about it and making out.

Men have always been expected to take the initiative in pursuing relationships. The man woos and courts while the woman sits sidesaddle in her salon chair, arranging and rearranging her petticoat ruffles. It's never the girl standing outside the boy's bedroom window holding up a boom box.

When it came to the physical relationship, it was the man's job to initiate first contact. If a woman demurred, it was not necessarily because she didn't want to say yes, but because saying yes without at least a pretense of resistance risked her reputation.

Back in ye olden days (and here I am referring to when I was growing up and earlier), both parties understood—or men *thought* they understood—that "no" was almost never to be taken at face value. No might mean no, but it also might mean maybe. No could even mean yes if you just kept kissing her. Look at any of those old movies where the hard-nosed detective finally kisses the dame he's been arguing with for the last two reels. He wraps her in his arms and plants a smooch right on her kisser. She resists, bats at him with her fists. He ignores her. Finally, she submits, returning his passion with hers.

Millions of us grew up with images like those. The message was clear: Even if she is punching you to get you to stop kissing her, all you have to do is persist. Eventually, she will come to realize it's what she wanted all along.

This ambiguity was considered a crucial part of sexual courtship. The boy persisted, the girl resisted. And then, somehow, love blossomed. It was that middle part I couldn't quite get my head around. How were we guys supposed to understand the difference between no no, maybe no, and yes no? Some guys adopted a sneering attitude toward girls, as if her disinterest in his pursuit could be overcome with the contemptuous line, "You know you want it."

But what if she didn't "want it"? How was a guy supposed to know, and how was a girl supposed to communicate it to him? Slowly, the phrase "no means no" began percolating through the culture, an effort to deliver to men the important message of consent. The only time I heard the word "consent" as a kid was when my mom signed permission slips for field trips.

"No means no" was born out of a time when the idea of consent was as malleable as a lump of Silly Putty. A guy just had to massage it into some recognizable shape and he was good to go. One of the most famous songs from my childhood was "Summer Lovin'" from the musical *Grease*, about two teenagers describing their summer fling and which includes the cheerful musical question, "Did she put up a fight?"

I hear that now and think, *What the fuck?* Guess what, Danny Zuko—if she's putting up a fight, you're raping her. In a 2018 article in *The Atlantic*, Megan Gerber describes the phrase "no means no" as a "[relic] of a time when 'don't rape women' was still treated as a moral argument rather than a moral fact."

She's right. We didn't talk about rape or sexual assault in anything close to the same terms that we talk about it now. My recollection of the attitudes toward sex crimes perpetrated by men against women was that they were bad things to do, yes, perhaps even jailable offenses, but also the sorts of things that inevitably happened when girls put themselves in situations in which they might occur. In other words, there was always a question of the female's culpability in the crime committed against her. If she got raped, it was a tragedy, but also, in a sense, a natural conclusion to a series of events in which she must have played no small part. Unlike any other crime, sexual assault is one in which the victim is assumed to share the blame. That tendency to victim-blame remains with us even today.

Amazingly, as "no means no" gained traction, it also found resistance. Even among women. To some women, the idea of explicit communication between men and women about their sexual boundaries stripped the mystery and allure from dating. The problem was, and to a certain extent remains, knowing the rules—rules that were never made explicit to me because the rules *weren't* explicit. They varied depending on the people and circumstances. Or maybe they only seemed to vary because, in actual fact, they didn't exist. The reason so many guys don't think they're guilty of sexual misconduct may be because, according to *their* rules—which is to say, the rules they set for themselves because nobody had ever clarified for them the basic idea of consent—they hadn't done anything wrong.

Laying down clear lines of consent diminishes the chances for misunderstanding or worse. Even today, the idea of asking for and receiving enthusiastic, affirmative consent still hasn't penetrated the skulls of some men. Here's an excerpt from an essay written by obscure "dating coach" Vincent Vinturi on his website, *Return of Kings*. I'm quoting it because, even though the dude and his site are obscure, the attitude is fairly representative of a lot of the kind of trash you'll find from the "alpha male" community, which celebrates aggressive male behavior and denigrates any guy who does not subscribe to it as a "beta male" or "cuck."

Ask any guy who's banged a lot of girls and has had a lot of same-night lays, and he will surely regale you with tales of seemingly insurmountable resistance, conquered and slain by his resolve and unwavering horniness. It's in the nature of beautiful women to resist, test, protest, sabotage and make your job of fucking them difficult.

Does that sound like a license to rape to you? Because it sure does to me. Yet the attitude behind this sentiment was common when I was growing up. Girls said no because they were teases. Girls said no because they were mean or vindictive. Girls said no because they were "bitches" or "dykes." Your job, as a guy, was to overcome their no.

You're entering a dating environment that, from the outside, seems more egalitarian than the one I encountered, but also far more perilous. There's a lot of guidance aimed at young women, words of sex-positivity, encouragement, and empowerment. The evidence suggests those messages are being received.

On the other hand, young men are being told, in some respects, to be *less* confident, *less* empowered. We're told we have an overabundance of those quali-ties, and we need to dial them back to ensure that the young women in our lives feel heard and respected. I suppose this is, generally speaking, good advice, but it also conflicts with behavior we still expect—and sometimes want—from men.

Are we still supposed to be confident, strong, and assertive? Or are we supposed to be sensitive, empathetic, and vulnerable? Can we be all of the above? How do we navigate the ungainly terrain between the traditional approach, in which men are expected to lead every aspect of courtship, and the new, bumpier landscape in which every step must be carefully measured, each new aspect of the relationship negotiated?

It's confusing for both sexes. I was speaking with a female executive who said, "It's hard because you want to be powerful, you want to be the boss. But you also want to be taken out to dinner."

Isn't that what we all want? To be tough at times, soft at times? To lead and to be led? These desires don't have to be exclusive. It's okay to want both. Sometimes you're the spooner and sometimes you're the spoonee.

Which is why I was so confused when I first started dating. I always went slow with my girlfriends. My hesitation was partly fear around creating offense and partly terrible self-doubt that made it nearly impossible for me to believe that a girl actually *wanted* me to make a move. Perhaps, I thought, she just enjoys hanging out in Denny's parking lots with guys in whom she has no interest.

I remember a huge clue that went right over my head right before I started dating my first girlfriend in high school. She and I took the train into New York one weekend in the late fall. At the time, we were kind of flirting with each other in school, maybe exchanging notes during class. Nothing had happened between us and I didn't know if her interest in me was anything but platonic. As we walked down Broadway on a chilly day, she looked at me and said, "My hand is cold . . ."

"Put it in your pocket," I responded, not realizing that she was trying to tell me she wanted me to hold her hand. Such. A. Doof.

Of course there will always be some ambiguity in a relationship, particularly in the beginning. Neither party wants to appear too forward only to get rejected. That part of the experience will probably never change and, honestly, it's fun. Flirting is fun. Taking tentative steps toward each other is fun. As you gain confidence in the dating world, you'll eventually get a sense of the right time to lean in for that first kiss. As you do, though, ask her if it's okay. "Can I kiss you?" does not have to be a buzzkill. If anything, it will enhance the moment when she says yes. And if she says no, congratulations! You've just avoided a sexual assault.

In other words, sex does not have to be some minefield you're attempting to cross without getting blown up. Far from it. Having consent frees you from the terror of wondering, "Is this okay?" and opens you to the experience of being honest, loving, and positive. Don't wait for her to say no; you should actively affirm that what's happening is what she wants to happen. Moreover, check in with yourself to make sure that what's happening is also what *you* want.

Traditional masculinity assumes that all guys are sex-crazed goons. We're not. Yes, we sometimes (often) want sex. But not always, and not always with the person who is offering it to us. I feel like this is an under-discussed aspect of male sexuality, but it's important. Men can say no, too. There may be times when you find yourself in a situation with somebody who wants a level of intimacy that, for whatever reason, you do not. Say no. Don't go through with it because you feel bad or you feel like it's what's expected of you, or you feel like somehow you will be less of a man if you do not. Just as a woman's body is hers to control, your body is yours to do with what you choose.

The other thing I want to tell you is that it's okay to want an emotional connection with somebody before you have sex with them. It's an obvious thing to say, but we tend to think of placing emotional intimacy before physical intimacy as a "girl thing" instead of a "human thing."

Personally, I have sometimes just wanted to have a purely physical relationship with somebody, and sometimes I have wanted something more. Either is okay. You're under no obligation to pursue sex for the sake of sex. Some guys do. Some girls do. That's all fine. The expectation with guys, though, is that we will always choose sex over intimacy. Don't believe it.

I generally regretted the few one-night stands I

had, not because they were "wrong," but because they didn't provide me with what I really wanted, which was a connection to somebody that extended past the physical. In the moment, it felt awesome to be wanted because I felt so insecure about my own self-worth that if somebody expressed desire in me, that was enough for me to desire them. But those moments didn't solve anything. They provided a temporary relief from my own insecurities, yes, but the end result often left me feeling worse. What was I doing with this person in my bed, or me in hers? There's a reason they call the next morning's departure the "walk of shame." Trust me, men feel that shame, too. We just don't talk about it. Because talking about our sexual shame *no es más macho.*

Again, I'm not making a judgment on spending a single night with somebody. But if you *are* going to have a one-night stand, it's vital that you communicate with each other that that's what you both are doing before you do it. Tell the person, "This is great. I'm happy we're doing this, but this is a one-night stand for me. If you're cool with that, let's keep going. If you're not, let's not."

Don't let other people dictate your comfort with sex. We're so conditioned to think of men as insatiable sexual carnivores that we don't allow for the possibility that they might be the one to delay or forego sex with somebody. If you do decide to move forward together, be kind. Ask. Listen. Treat "no means no" as an inviolable rule. I know I've said it already, but it's worth repeating: If she wants to stop for any reason, stop. Same goes for you. If you want to stop for any reason, stop. Your mind and body are your own to do with as you see fit. Be respectful, be patient with your partners. Be as attuned to your partner as you are to yourself. Maybe more so.

Imagine how scary it might be for a woman to go to somebody's place, maybe a little inebriated, take off all her clothes, and open her body to a person who is probably bigger, heavier and stronger than she is. Men don't generally think about these things because they don't have to. Women have to. They always have to.

"There's always a level of fear involved," Mom says when I ask her about her early experiences with men.

"You feel like you have to be constantly vigilant because you *do*. It's just a fact."

If we want women to control their own sexuality (and it's worth mentioning that there are many, many men in this world who absolutely do *not* want that), then we have to understand that they are usually going to be more vulnerable in sexual situations than guys. They will always be taking more of a gamble than men because women are more likely to suffer adverse consequences for engaging in sex. Anything from getting pregnant to catching an STD or being physically assaulted. Even their reputation may be put at risk for simply wanting to connect with somebody.

Although the larger culture is growing more welcoming of female sexuality, it's still true that women often face judgment for their sexual appetites in ways that men do not. Women are shamed for having sex, and shamed for not having sex. When you consider everything they have to put up with, it's amazing women want to have sex with men at all.

Sex should be a joy. It should be fun and it should

connect you with somebody. It will be none of those things if it ever feels coerced. Not all sex has to have love, but all sex has to have consent.

Here's something else that nobody talks about because it flies in the face of every cultural message we receive: sex isn't that important.

As guys, we're taught that sex is always the goal. In so many ways, we're taught that our self-worth as guys hinges on the question of how many people will have sex with us. When I was a few years older than you are right now, my friends and I had our first TV show on the air. We were young and popular and all I wanted to do was figure out how to convert the currency of my new fame into having sex with girls. I'd go out to bars (where I didn't drink) to try to meet girls (in whom I didn't have much interest) and stay out until three or four o'clock in the morning (well after I wanted to be asleep) in the hope that somebody—anybody—would want to have sex with me. As I said, the few times an evening like that ended with a one-night stand left me feeling somehow worse. I'd accomplished my "goal," but over time I learned that the goal itself was misplaced, that I was looking for something else that I didn't have the words for. I have the word now. It's "intimacy."

Looking back, I think sex represented a space for me that allowed me to be a more open version of myself than I generally allowed myself to be. In those darkened bedrooms, I could be playful, tough, and vulnerable all at the same time. I could fully engage with somebody in a way that felt impossible in any other situation. My day-to-day life as a guy felt so closed off, sardonic, constrained. When I was with somebody, though, I felt as though I could be a fuller, more open me. Afterward, that more open person faded away as the same need for validation and acceptance that brought me to that person's bed in the first place returned. My morning walk of shame wasn't about doing something shameful; it was about being somebody I didn't much like in the first place.

What I'm offering here is, I hope, a more nuanced take on sex than you're getting from the culture. Your sexual life is yours alone. You can do with it what you want. You can have as much or as little sex as you want with however many or few people as you choose. Especially in the beginning, though, I would advise you to go slow and to make sure you're having sex with the right person for the right reasons. Let those reasons be based on something more than lust. And, for God's sake, wear a condom.

THIRTEEN

Everything and Nothing

Be Humane

A COMEDIAN I know named Michelle Buteau has a joke about never farting in front of her husband. "I've been holding in a fart for ten years!" she says. It's funny because, duh, farts are funny. The reason the joke lands, though, is because her underlying premise rings true: women are often reluctant to display their fullest selves in front of their male partners because if they were to show the actual messy business of being a person, men would find them repugnant.

Here's a much more acidic version of almost the same sentiment. Journalist Talia Lavin once wrote, "Most men do not think women are fully human. And 'most' is generous."

It's a startling and awful thing to say, and it really nagged at me the first time I read it. The more I've thought about it, however, the more I've come to believe she's right.

That being said, I don't necessarily agree with the sentiment in the way that she framed it. My interpretation is that she's saying most men view women as *lesser* creatures than themselves. I don't believe that's true for most men (although I'm sure an alarmingly high number of men think exactly that). Instead, I think men and women are raised to believe that we are slightly *different* species altogether, like black bears and brown bears. Both are bears, but they each get their own Latin name.

The sexes are raised to regard each other as distinct. There's even that little nursery rhyme about it:

> Snips and snails, and puppy-dog's tails,
> That's what little boys are made of.
> Sugar and spice and all things nice,
> That's what little girls are made of.

I mean, what is *that* shit? Girls are made from "all things nice"? You and I both know your sister. One of you got the lion's share of snips and snails—and it wasn't you. I say that, of course, with tremendous love and affection for your sister, whom I love nearly as much as you. (And now, of course, I have to clarify that I am joking about loving you more than your sister when we both know I love her more.)

Lavin's argument that men don't see women as fully human isn't new. In a 1792 essay "A Vindication of the Rights of Woman," an English writer and philosopher named Mary Wollstonecraft made the same point, writing that men regard "females as women rather than as human creatures."

Which makes me wonder: If a woman isn't a "human creature," then what is she? Some separate category of being? Conversely, it asks and answers its own implied question: If a woman isn't a human being, then who is? A man, of course, and only a man.

Historically, this distinction has served us men very well. After all, if men are one thing and women another, it stands to reason that each should be assigned different tasks accordingly. Men are "logical" and "strong," for example, while women are "emotional" and "delicate." It doesn't take much imagination to see how rigid ideas like these would, and could, be used to keep women subservient. The underlying message to women: you are not enough. In the end, this results in a terrible disconnect between the sexes, a disconnect that encourages us to think of others' life experiences, their humanity, as different from our own.

No wonder Michelle Buteau doesn't feel like she can fart in front of her husband.

I would ask some follow-up questions to Lavin's statement: If men do not view women as fully human, how do we view other members of our own sex? Do men grant *other men* the same unconditional humanity that we grant ourselves? In other words, do men treat other men more *humanely* than we treat women?

No.

The word "humane" has an almost comic lack of self-awareness. We use it to connote benevolence and compassion, as if those attributes are closer to our true natures than malevolence and indifference. History and a casual perusal of the day's news will tell you that isn't the case. So what is the "true" nature of our species? Why do we so often behave one way with one group of people and an entirely different way with another?

In *Sapiens: A Brief History of Humankind*, Yuval Noah Harari explains that prehistoric people evolved to function in small groups, or "bands," each band containing a few dozen people at most. Although different bands may have cooperated with each other at times, there's no reason to believe they granted each other the same rights and privileges afforded to their own groups. In other words, they may not have treated each other as "fully human."

As we've developed language, technology, and organizational structures, he argues, we've gone from small groups in which everybody personally knows each other to massive, global groups in which hardly any members have personal relationships. A Muslim in Syria is unlikely to know a Muslim in Indiana, but they will recognize each other as belonging to the same "band" known as Muslims. Or a Nike employee in Holland may not know one in India, but both draw their paychecks from the same company, and both have an interest in that company's success. Every single one of us belongs to dozens, maybe hundreds, of these kinds of groupings. Often, the way we treat each other depends on how close or far away we view the other person's band from our own. Your allegiance to the other members of your band can grow greater or more tenuous as you zoom in and out.

For example, you and I are both Americans. We're likely to have an affinity for other Americans. Because of this affinity, you'd expect that we would treat other Americans in the same way that we would expect to be treated ourselves. But there are innumerable and obvious ways that we Americans create distinctions that limit the ways we practice equality. We may say we believe that all Americans are entitled to the same rights, a sentiment literally written into our founding document. Yet our history has shown us time and again that this isn't—and never has been—the case. Instead, we reserve certain rights and privileges for people of a certain gender, skin tone, and level of wealth. Every American understands, for example, that a poor black woman has fewer resources to petition her government than a wealthy white man. She has fewer opportunities for educational advancement, medical care, and financial stability than her wealthier white male peers. That is the nature of our American culture, a culture that says "all men are created equal" but does not fulfill the promise of that slogan.

We live in a power structure that, traditionally, values men over women, and certain men over other men. When we talk about whom we treat as fully human, I agree with Lavin's broad point, but I think she could extend her point to include two other categories that explain who gets afforded "equal treatment" and who does not.

The great feminist thinker and writer bell hooks (she spells her name with lowercase letters like e e cummings) talks about how our American system is not purely, or even primarily, about sex. Instead, she talks about the "interrelatedness of race, sex, and class oppression"—or what you and your classmates call "intersectionality"—as the organizing principles around which our culture revolves. I think she's right, and I think she's right to order it in the way that she does.

The people at the top of our power structure are wealthy white men. Although these men have always dominated the upper echelons, they've always been accompanied by (almost exclusively) white women. Most of these women have been spouses or family members. Although the women may not have had as much power as the men, they certainly possessed far more status and power than men of lower social classes. As the culture opened up in the last half century or so, more women found themselves moving up the power structure independently of the men in their lives. These women continue to be predominantly white. While there are far more of these women than ever before, the top ranks of our system continue to be occupied mostly by white men.

At the bottom of our social system, we find a preponderance of people of color, especially African

Americans. Often women. Always poor. What we see is that it is far more difficult for people possessing the "wrong" color skin and gender to move upward in this power structure. Think about the opening lines from *Hamilton* in which composer Lin-Manuel Miranda asks how a "bastard, orphan, son of a whore" from an obscure Caribbean island grows up to be a hero and scholar, "the ten-dollar Founding Father."

The answer is that it's always been easier to overcome low social class than skin color or gender. Hamilton's story is unlikely, yes, but at that time he could not have risen to such heights if he'd been a black man or a woman. Again, think of our structure as based first on race, then gender, then class.

Does the example of Barack Obama belie this ordering? Perhaps. After all, if race were the primary determinant of our choices, we would have expected to see a white woman elected president before an African American man. True enough, but I think it's important to recognize that what is generally true isn't always true. Consider how often over the centuries white women have been privileged over non-white people. Consider

how much more extraordinary Barack Obama was—
and had to be—compared to so many of the men who
held the job, including the man who preceded him,
George W. Bush.

When a (white) woman finally secured the
Democratic nomination for president, it was fascinat-
ing to look at the way women voted. During the 2016
presidential campaign, political analysts assumed that
women would vote for Hillary Clinton over Donald
Trump because they thought female voters would pri-
oritize their gender over other considerations. To a
certain extent, the analysts were correct: 54 percent of
women did vote for Hillary Clinton, but that number is
the percentage of women *overall* who voted for Clinton.
Donald Trump actually received the majority of *white*
women's votes.

It's kind of startling to realize that a male presidential candidate credibly accused of sexual harassment,
assault, and misbehavior by two dozen women won
more votes from white women than the female candidate who spent decades working on specific issues
related to women's health and economic empowerment.

Why?

Why would white women vote for a candidate who seemed to embody the awful, boorish behavior so many of them have been subjected to throughout their lives? Why would they vote for somebody who seemed to be actively working *against* the best interests of their sex?

It starts to make sense if you keep in mind hooks' ordering of the power structure, which places race at the top. You know how the singer Michael Bublé takes old musical standards and repackages them for a new audience? That's what Trump did with racism. After launching his campaign with the racist "birther" smear against Barack Obama, he then based his winning presidential campaign on dehumanizing Spanish-speaking and Muslim immigrants. It worked well enough that white women prioritized their racial fears over whatever gender concerns they may have had about Donald Trump.

(By the way, I'm not knocking Michael Bublé. Mom thinks he's terrific. By law, all middle-aged white women from Connecticut are required to like Michael Bublé.)

That's the status quo. We call this ordering system a bunch of different things, some of them more neutral-sounding than others. "Americanism" sounds a whole lot better than "patriarchy," which sounds a whole lot better than "white supremacy." Whatever you want to call it, this system instituted race as the animating force of American life. Happily, and inevitably, as our demographics shift, those racial conventions are changing. More men and women of color are rising through the power structure. Women, racial minorities, members of the LGBTQ community—all have made tremendous gains over the last few decades. But yesterday's progress takes a long time to become today's status quo.

Lately, there has been strong resistance to any change in the status quo. We're seeing attempts to roll back civil rights gains on every front: from voting restrictions, to reproductive constraints, to the ban on transgender troops serving in the military, to an overreaching "Muslim ban," to punitive immigration policies. All of these regressive steps are designed to protect a recalcitrant status quo.

Will the regressive voices succeed, or will the long arc of the moral universe continue to bend, as Martin Luther King Jr. once said, toward justice? And what does all of this have to do with you, eighteen years old, one foot out the door?

Everything. And nothing.

Part of the reason it's so hard to talk about how to be a better man is that our manhood doesn't exist in isolation from our race or our social class. This is why the conversation about masculinity gets so difficult. Because when you talk about one thing—how we become better men—you almost immediately have to talk about everything else. You have to talk about class differences and racism and misogyny. They're all so deeply entwined that it's impossible to disentangle any of these from the others.

Slavery was an economic decision, for example, which attempted to justify its inhumanity through racism, which, in turn, leaned on pseudoscience and religion to bolster its legitimacy. How do you separate any of these things? You can't.

Power seems to have its own gravity. It accrues

bits of this and that through the force of its own mass. Eventually, we walk along its surface without even realizing that it's holding us down. That's the situation we currently find ourselves facing. We're so ensnared by this vast power that many of us don't even recognize its force. Why would we? For people like you and me, it may even feel like a force for good. After all, we're housed and fed and warm. Our family is generally treated with respect. I make money. You spend the money I make. We do okay.

But for others, patriarchy is a crushing force that doesn't allow them to rise up as far as they might go. Many people have to work so much harder than those born into fortunate circumstances just to have the chance that you and I assume is ours by birthright. White, middle-class kids born into this system are granted far more opportunities than their poorer black or Latino or Native American counterparts.

The racial component is as enmeshed into this system as the gender component. So when I talk about becoming "a better man," I am specifically talking about becoming a better *white* man because I feel a responsibility as the beneficiary of this system to do what I can to expand opportunities within this system. And I want you to feel this, too. Your privilege ends up being a double-edged sword. You have been given as many opportunities as anybody could hope to have, but the tradeoff is that you must use some of that privilege to help other people. That's a responsibility you inherit along with the color of your skin. I don't mean just donating money, although that can certainly be helpful. I mean, in your life, choosing to participate in the sometimes uncomfortable work of confrontation and resistance. You may not want to. You may hate to do it because those who would rather you just kept your mouth shut might give you the stink-eye. I'm telling you, though, you have to do it.

Although you are only half Jewish, your Jewishness also carries with it some special responsibilities. One of the interesting aspects of being Jewish is feeling, on some level, that you are part of the white American class, but also slightly apart from it. It's like, we pass because they let us pass, but our "whiteness" always feels conditional. In fact, it's an anti-Semitic trope that

Jews aren't white at all. Whenever some Nazi wannabe sends me trash like that on Twitter, I don't know whether to feel offended or flattered.

Jews have always struggled with our place in American culture. We've worried about appearing *too* Jewish for fear of standing out. It's why I changed my name from Schwartz to Black. When becoming an actor, I didn't want people to think of me as "Jewish" from the moment I walked into a casting office. I wanted something more neutral. Actually, more "white." Since "schwartz" means "black," I decided to go with it. I used to have a joke in which I said I changed my name because I was "ashamed of being Jewish," and there was definitely a kernel of truth to that. It's the same reason I feel a little worried when I see groups of Hasidic Jews in Brooklyn, their peculiar and defiant dress and style standing out against the contemporary city backdrop. Part of me can't help worrying whether they're standing out too much, drawing too much attention to themselves, and that, in doing so, they put all of us at risk. That's what two thousand years of paranoia will do to you.

Yet here we are, largely accepted in the most powerful country in the world. We have made outsized contributions to that country relative to our numbers. We've done this, I suspect, to attempt to make ourselves indispensable, to prove that we belong.

Of course, it doesn't entirely work. Year after year, Jews are the single most targeted religious group in the country, and anti-Semitic attacks are on the rise here and abroad. According to the Anti-Defamation League, 2017 was the worst year for American anti-Semitic attacks on record. So we live in an in-between state, belonging and not quite belonging, all of us harboring the slight suspicion that we may be nothing more than guests in our own home.

All of this to say that our history as Jews gives you additional responsibilities to other people. First, we are obliged to lift others up as a recognition of the privilege we've been afforded. Second, we are obliged to speak up on behalf of others as a recognition of the history our people endured when few people spoke up for us. I will be the first to admit that I have not done enough to lift people up. As I've gotten older, and my recognition of my responsibilities has grown, I have tried to do more. I will continue to do more.

At the very least, it means speaking up on behalf of women and minorities. It means checking your friends when they say demeaning or degrading shit. It means being willing to step into a confrontation to help another person. Simple stuff. But it's the kind of stuff so many men often fail to do. You do not need to sneak downstairs in the middle of the night to be brave. Sometimes all it requires is speaking up.

Once you are aware of your own privileges, whatever they may be, you must consider them and act accordingly. That's not a judgment of you, only an acknowledgment of what is true. For example, sociologist Michael Kimmel recounts a conversation he overheard once between a white woman and a black woman:

The black woman says to the white woman, "When you wake up in the morning and you look in the mirror, what do you see?" And the white woman said, "I see a woman." And the black woman said, "You see, that's the problem for me. Because when I wake up in the morning and I look in the mirror, I see a black woman. To me, race is visible, but to you it's invisible. You don't see it." And then she said something really startling. She said, "That's how privilege works. Privilege is invisible to those who have it."

That's all I'm doing here, trying to make the invisible visible. Once you see it, you can't unsee it, as much as you might like to. Also, once you see it, that doesn't mean you see *all* of it. You can't, any more than a human eye can see the entire spectrum of light. The rest of the spectrum is out there, but your personal experiences only equip you to see a narrow band. When others better equipped than you tell you what's out there beyond your vision, believe them.

And I know how sick to death white guys are of hearing about their "white male privilege," but however sick white guys might be hearing about it, imagine being on the other side of that privilege. Imagine not being given the benefit of the doubt, or being thought of as less than, or fearing for your safety because of your sex or your race. A white NBA player named Kyle Korver wrote an essay examining his own racial privilege, how he thinks he's let some of his black teammates down over the years, and how he's resolved to be a better teammate and man:

> What I'm realizing is, no matter how passionately I commit to being an ally, and no matter how unwavering my support is for NBA and WNBA players of color . . . I'm still in this conversation from the privileged perspective of opting in to it. Which of course means that on the flip side, I could just as easily opt out of it. Every day, I'm given that choice—I'm granted that privilege—based on the color of my skin.

The privilege is also true for our sex and class. As guys, we get to opt in or out of these conversations because we don't have to handle the daily indignities that come from occupying a less privileged place. You're a relatively well-off white boy from Connecticut. It's on you to figure out how you want to handle the perks that come with that position.

One way to deal with it is to ignore it. Perhaps you feel like these issues don't impact you directly, so why should you care? You may feel it's not your responsibility to fix what you did not break. That may be true to a certain extent, but I also think when you do not make an effort to fix what you know to be broken, you are actively making things worse for everybody else. It's a choice, but remember how I said our debts tether us to other people? This is one of your debts. Moreover, selfishness won't set you free from your obligations. It may forestall them, but you cannot escape your own humanity. At some point, you will have to figure out how you want to handle your responsibilities to other people.

I can't tell you how to do that. But I can tell you that you're not applying for sainthood here. You don't need to be all things to all people. You don't need to address every issue or solve every problem. You just need to help out a little bit. You may find that the more you do, the more you *want* to do. If so, cool. There is always more to do. You don't have to do all of it, but you have to do some. Recognizing the shared humanity of others allows you to become fully human yourself. That is being humane.

FOURTEEN

Here I Am

Do Something Positive

EARLIER, I SAID that you shouldn't have to be exceptional to succeed in this life. That's true. It's also true that there will always be exceptional women and men who rise above difficult circumstances to achieve great things. Exceptional people will find a way to succeed no matter what because they are, by definition, exceptional. But consider all the unexceptional people who wind up in positions of power and authority. I am one of them. Although my power and authority are pretty limited, I'm still writing these words from a house that Mom and I built with the money I earned telling jokes on TV. Even to me, that seems absurd. How did that even happen?

I can tell you exactly: I was born into the middle class within a family that valued education. I had access to decent public schools. My father had the foresight and resources to purchase life insurance. When he died, the vast bulk of that money went to your aunt Susan but enough of it went to your uncle Eric and me that we would be able to get through college with minimal debt. I attended an exclusive private college, NYU, and I joined a sketch comedy troupe where we had the luxury to devote all of our free time to learning how to write and perform comedy. One of our members had an unpaid internship (he came from a wealthy family who could subsidize that unpaid internship) at MTV, where he knew a producer because his sister had dated him years before. That producer brought our sketch group into the network, where we were given an opportunity to work on a TV show. Based on the success of our work on that show, our group was given a show of our own.

Without my even trying very hard, I suddenly had a show on one of the hottest networks on television. We worked hard to get that opportunity, yes, but none of that preliminary work would have been possible without the special privileges every single one of us brought with us to NYU. None of us had to work full-time to pay for college, for example. None of us had kids or arrest records or had to care for younger siblings. Only two out of eleven of us came from divorced families, and I was the only one who had a lost a parent in childhood.

In fact, I walk around all the time with the guilt that my father's death actually enabled my success at NYU because, while he was alive, he always told my brother and me that he was going to send us to New Jersey's state school, Rutgers. Maybe that would have been great and maybe not, but without the life insurance money, I wouldn't have been able to afford NYU. Had he not died, I wouldn't have met the people with whom I started my career.

There is nothing exceptional about me. Yes, I was smart *enough*, talented and ambitious *enough*. But I wasn't special. None of us were. Yet there we were, in our early twenties, with our own hit show on MTV.

(And, by the way, our comedy group had 10 white guys and 1 white girl.)

What does all this mean for you? To be honest, I don't really know. It's not a guilt trip. It's just to make the point that we are all both deserving and undeserving of the good fortune we receive. Most of us are ordinary people. Whether we end up "deserving" our successes in life is hard to say. It's not a knock on myself to say I got lucky, and I'm not trying to make you feel bad for being born into good fortune. If anything, I'm thrilled for you and thrilled for myself that I've been able to provide you and your sister with a good home and food and experiences beyond the grasp of so many. It's not that I feel like I don't deserve it, but rather I recognize that I don't deserve it any more than so many other people who end up with so much less. So I guess what I'm offering here is a caution.

First, I'm cautioning you against entitlement, which really is the bane of white people in general, and white dudes in particular. I don't think most of us even realize the extent of our entitlement. It manifests itself in the confident way we enter a store, for example, when we expect to be welcomed as potential customers instead of eyed as potential shoplifters, even though I used to regularly shoplift when I lived in New York.

I used to steal food, compact discs, little geegaws that caught my eye in boutiques. I did it for the thrill of it and yes, eventually I got caught. A plainclothes security officer caught me stuffing a Miles Davis CD into my pants. I was let off with a warning instead of an arrest. Was that white privilege? You bet your ass it was. Imagine if I'd been a poor black kid getting caught for the same. Maybe I would have been let off with the same warning. Maybe not. How do we measure luck? Sometimes it's by the color of our skin.

Our entitlement may express itself in the way we use our voice in conversation, assured that our opinion will be valued or that we know more about any given subject than our listener. Or maybe it expresses itself in how we deal with authority and, more importantly, how authority deals with us.

I was listening to a story on the podcast *Serial* about a woman who got into a bar fight. When she was arrested, she started drunkenly screaming at the arresting officer, kicking the police car from inside, and generally making a nuisance of herself. The interviewer, Sarah Koenig, asked her why she thought she could talk to cops like that. The woman responded, somewhat ruefully, "I hate to say—I'm a white girl."

While I obviously don't encourage this form of entitlement, I also disagree with those who say, "You're not entitled to anything." Of course you are. You're entitled to a lot of things: we've got a whole fancy constitution spelling out exactly what those things are. Beyond your constitutionally enumerated entitlements, I believe you are also entitled to respect, and I expect you to treat others with respect. You are entitled to control over your own body, and I expect you to honor other people's control of their bodies. Further, you are entitled to your own thoughts, which is to say you are entitled to keep your own counsel about all things regardless of what anybody tells you is so. Keeping your own counsel, however, is not an excuse for ignorance; I expect you to seek out the knowledge you need in order to understand your own mind. A healthy sense of entitlement is good, the kind that protects your dignity and self-worth. Unhealthy entitlement is the sort that makes you believe you are privileged above others.

A lot of times that kind of entitlement is hard to recognize. Be mindful of it in yourself and others. If somebody tells you that you are acting in an entitled manner, believe them. They may not always be correct, but at least entertain the possibility that they see something in you that you're unable to see in yourself.

In general, even if we see it, white people rarely admit our own entitlement. We understand that our travels through society will never be inhibited by the color of our skin. Moreover, we also understand that somebody else's journey may be inhibited by the color of *their* skin. We get all of it but we don't like to admit it because, when the sailing is smooth, we tend to think it's because we are great sailors when, in fact, it might just be that we've got the wind at our back.

A different shade of entitlement is when we mistake confidence for competence. Let your confidence grow from inside out, not outside in. Boys have a tendency to overvalue their abilities, whereas girls are more likely to undervalue theirs. Girls are more likely to acknowledge their shortcomings and to ask for help to address them, whereas guys tend to try to muscle through problems on our own. You're entitled to ask for help.

You're also entitled to make mistakes. Everybody is. The *privilege* you have is that the mistakes *you* make are likely to be less costly than the mistakes of people without your privilege because you have a vast support system in place (everything from me and your mom to a legal system that favors white guys who can afford good lawyers). Is that fair? Of course not. I'm just pointing out that our system is designed to help people like us, and so I would caution you against judging the mistakes of others too harshly—they could just as easily be your own.

Some men have fought for greater inclusion because, aside from the basic morality of it, they hope that creating more opportunities for everybody will eventually lead to greater opportunities for all. On the other hand, many guys resist helping others because they fear the gains of others will come at their expense. I see this in my own little comedy community.

Comedy has always been dominated by white dudes, but the past few years have upended that power structure. The days of the all-male writers' room, for example, are probably over. Does that mean the comedy world is now suddenly "fair"? Not even remotely. But maybe it's getting fairer. This new push for inclusion doesn't mean talented white men won't keep getting work. Of course they will. But it does mean that guys with average abilities who might have gotten the job before may not get the job now because they're competing with a broader talent pool. In some cases, they may actually be at a disadvantage because writers' rooms are trying to ensure that more voices are represented. That's going to scare some guys. Honestly, as one of those comedy writers with average abilities, it scares *me*.

Acting, too. There's a far more diverse group of entertainers on our televisions, tablets, and movie screens than we've ever seen. Do they perfectly mirror our culture? Of course not. But this new inclusion almost certainly means less work for schlubby white character actors like me. Is it *a lot* less work or *a little* less work? It's hard to say, but, again, I would be lying if I said I'm not a little scared. I certainly never felt entitled to writing or acting jobs, but now that I'm having a harder time finding that work, it stings. So no, you shouldn't have to be exceptional to succeed in life, but some of us who have been coasting on our mediocrity may have to up our game in order to stay afloat.

I'm one white guy in one "liberal" industry. I've done well enough for myself. Even acknowledging my own "economic anxiety" seems ridiculous compared to all the other men out there in all the other industries trying, like polar bears on ever-shrinking ice patches, to hold their ground. One way or another, I'll be fine. Even so, I worry about my ability to continue to provide. And, of course, I worry about you.

You're heading off to study videogame design, which probably feels exactly as realistic to me as it must have seemed to my mom when I told her I was going to New York to study acting. And, truthfully, you probably have as much idea about what it means to be a videogame designer as I did about what it meant to be an actor—slim to none.

Maybe your career path will work out for you. Maybe it won't. Maybe you'll get ten years into it and decide to do something else. In the end, I don't think it matters that much. Too many of us measure our masculinity by our occupation. Our income. The fluttering prestige of the meaningless.

You don't have to fall for it. Earlier, I talked about how we steer boys toward occupations instead of toward happiness, often equating one with the other. "What do you want to be when you grow up?" is not the same question as "What do you think will give you the most happiness?"

Happiness may feel like an ephemeral target, but it's not. I talked about happiness a little bit before, but I want to drill down into it. Happiness has three components: identity, community, and purpose. A job may provide some of that or none of it. There are happy people who dislike their jobs and unhappy people who identify strongly with their work. Maybe the reason they're unhappy is because they identify *too* strongly with their jobs. The best you can hope for, I think, is to find work you believe to be meaningful among people you enjoy being around. For most of my career, I've been fortunate enough to have that. I wish the same for you.

My own job has given me a community I adore. Despite the stereotype of actors being airheads, they actually tend to be smart, inquisitive, and empathetic. And despite the stereotype of comedians being depressive misanthropes, they're actually depressive misanthropes—so I guess that one is a little more accurate. But, again, they also tend to be smart, inquisitive, and empathetic. These communities have given me great friendships. At times, they've given me purpose. As I've gotten older, though, I find they provide less and less of an identity. When people ask me what I do, I often want to say, "I take a lot of naps," because napping feels as relevant to my larger identity as acting or doing stand-up or whatever else I find myself doing on any given day. Now that I think of it, I look forward to napping as much doing those other things (often more).

That's not to say I don't enjoy my job, but my purpose now isn't nearly as entwined with my occupation as it was when I was your age. Back then, I was so desperate to be "an actor" that I made myself, literally, sick. I fell into deep depressions because I focused my identity so narrowly on career advancement that any misstep or disappointment would send me into what felt, at times, like an irretrievable blackness.

At some point, you will almost certainly feel let down by the world. On the other hand, you may feel you've gotten more than you deserve. I hope you can learn to hold your gratitude tighter than your resentment. It's hard to remember sometimes (all the time) that the world spins neither for your benefit nor for your detriment. Each of us is here by some unknown grace. We don't have to understand how or why to feel humbled and appreciative. It's a gift, that's all, sent by a secret admirer.

Last night we had a family dinner out on the patio. Grilled salmon and salad. Mom had you running in and out of the house for plates and platters and silverware and the big glass water pitcher. Finally, after about a dozen trips, we were ready to eat. You sat down and jokingly muttered, "Here I am," as if the trips back and forth from the kitchen had left you disoriented. It made me laugh because I know the feeling of not knowing how you ended up anyplace at all. Here you are. Dig in.

◆◆◆◆

FIFTEEN

A Better Man

Breathe

IF YOU THINK if I'm starting to get a little woo-woo on you, don't worry—it's about to get worse. It's impossible to talk about your full life as a man without touching on your spiritual life.

As you know, I don't practice any religion and I don't believe in God, or at least I've never found a satisfactory definition of God in which to believe. At the same time, I'm uncomfortable describing myself as either an agnostic, which sounds too wishy-washy, or as an atheist, which sounds too definitive. Sometimes I jokingly refer to myself as a "praytheist," which I define as someone who prays to a god in which he does not believe, hoping to find evidence for God's existence, which he will then dismiss.

My faith in a higher power may be limited, but I am not without belief in the ineffable. I believe in the spirit, which I'll define as a person's animating force. Some people might use the words "spirit" and "soul" interchangeably when they talk about this stuff, but I'm going to stick with "spirit," because I think "soul" has some unnecessary moral weight that sits aside from what I'm going to tell you.

God, I think, is a creation of the spirit rather than the other way around.

Saying a higher power is necessary for me to believe in spirit is like saying I need God to believe in my own stomach. Not really. I have a stomach and I have a spirit. Questioning the existence of either seems pointless to me, as does the debate about how either of them got there. What's important to me is that I have a responsibility to keep both in good working order. Depriving either of nourishment will kill you just the same.

Just as we describe our want of food as hunger, we describe our want of spiritual food as "spiritual hunger," which we feed in service of our "spiritual needs." Both of those terms feel accurate to me because they carry the same imperative as food. We don't even have a phrase to describe this work as being optional, which is why there's no such thing as "spiritual wants."

I wonder if those needs get more pronounced as we age. I used to think people have a tendency to get more religious as they get older because they're hedging their bets with God as they get closer to death, but maybe that's not the case. Instead, maybe it's just part of our human design that the spirit grows louder as the body begins to quiet. Or maybe the spirit runs at the same volume throughout our lives, but we hear it more acutely once the noise of our lives has settled enough for us to finally listen to the forever questions of life and loss. How do we tune in to that voice?

Religion is often the nearest tool at hand.

Most people just kind of go along with whichever religion they are born into, the same way some people become Red Sox fans because that's the team their family rooted for. It always seems kind of funny to me, though, when people born into a particular religion believe that theirs is the "correct" one. To say that one religion is the one true religion is exactly the same as saying the Red Sox are the one true baseball team. It's absurd, especially since everybody knows that honor belongs to the Yankees.

You were born into two faiths, Catholicism and Judaism. At the moment, you don't identify with either of them very strongly, which is fine. Maybe you never will. Maybe you'll try out one or the other in adulthood. Or another still. To me, religions are more or less equal. I have attended services in several, and found myself inspired and moved by all. I would even consider joining a religion myself if it demanded neither a faith in God nor participatory singing.

If you do find religion one day, great. If you don't, also great. I would caution you, though, that your religious life and your spiritual life are related, but different, subjects. Becoming a member of a religion may guide your spiritual life, but it won't, by itself, solve whatever spiritual problems you encounter. Religion provides a framework, but you still have to do the work. It's like going to the gym. They give you the equipment, but it won't do you any good if you never break a sweat.

So what is that work? What feeds our spiritual hunger? To me, the work of the spirit is twofold. The first is discovering meaning and purpose: what inspires you, excites you, moves you, prods you to look more deeply into yourself? The answers to these questions will probably change over time. Spending a childhood building Thomas the Tank Engine train tracks can be just as spiritual as an adulthood poring over the Torah. Whatever connects you to yourself and inspires you is spiritual work.

The second, critical, part of your spiritual work is passing your inspiration on to others. A full spirit wants to be shared. The word "spirit" is a word for air, originating from the Latin *spiritus*, which means "breath." You can't hold your spirit any more than you can hold a lungful of air. Eventually, it has to be released. If you look at it that way, the machinery of the spirit seems simple enough: we inhale inspiration and exhale it back into the world.

Why don't most of us place a higher priority on our spiritual needs? Turn on the TV and you'll see pills for restless leg syndrome but nothing for a restless spirit, except the occasional commercial for Scientology. (Don't join Scientology.) Or maybe the better way to put it is that *everything* is being peddled as a cure for a restless spirit. We rarely frame consumerism as a spiritual pursuit, but that's exactly what it is, a faith that accumulating enough stuff will eventually quiet the jackhammer in our head.

Here's a bit of copy from the website for an air freshener: "Take a drive with the soothing scent of a Febreze One Bamboo Car Vent Clip. It'll make any commute a little calmer." How hollowed out by life do you have to be in order to believe that plugging a cartridge of hydroxypropyl beta-cyclodextrin into the air-conditioning vent is going to help *anything*?

Everybody already understands consumerism's empty promise, yet we can't rid ourselves of the habit of accumulation, just like most of us can't wean ourselves off sugar. And yes, you would be right to point out my own hypocrisy on this subject. One look around our house will confirm I'm as addicted to stuff as anybody else. I have three sets of silverware. Six nearly identical gray sweaters. Hundreds of books I will almost certainly never read. I am forever preaching to everybody in our household that we all need less. Yet I'm telling you right now: if I see a cool new gray sweater on sale at Banana Republic, I'm buying it. Why? Because *that's* the gray sweater purchase that will absolutely, definitely, 100 percent finally make me happy.

Why do we persist in this delusion? I don't know. Maybe it's just our primitive brains telling us to hoard sweaters in case of a sweater shortage. Maybe we're just dumb.

I'm not suggesting you live an ascetic life, only that you follow a practice of consideration. You're not always going to make good decisions one way or the other. Nobody does. If you get into the habit of consideration, hopefully you'll improve your average a little bit.

What do I mean by a "habit of consideration"? Just that. Taking a breath to consider. A check-in with yourself. How am I? What's going on with me? What am I doing right now, and why? Who or what am I serving?

Little moments of deliberation that will hopefully lead you to sound decisions about the choices you make day to day, moment to moment.

What does all of this have to do with masculinity? A lot, I think. Men and women are no different when it comes to spiritual matters. Every person feeds their spirit in different ways, but I suspect that women, on average, have greater access to their inner lives for the same reasons that they have greater access to their emotional lives. Not because they are naturally more open to their inner selves, but because we men are unnaturally closed off from our own. Men often end up stifling the best parts of our selves—our joy, our wonder, our empathy—to maintain our place in a pecking order that serves no purpose.

Your life will be immeasurably better if you can receive the gifts of the world: beauty, wonder, delight (I might also throw in "pizza"). It will be better still if you can accept those gifts and then pass them on. When we talk about traditional masculinity, we talk about strength, courage, aggression, independence. As I've said, there's nothing inherently wrong with any of those traits, but they'll prove meaningless to you if they aren't in the service of something greater.

Life, a good life, demands constant self-interrogation. Who am I? What do I value? Where do I devote my time? What deserves my attention? Be a relentless interrogator of yourself. Discover your own assumptions and question them. Question everything. Follow those lines of inquiry. Educate yourself. Find viewpoints that challenge your own and treat them with the seriousness that you would expect others to treat yours. Pick up books (yes, actual books). Read about other people's experiences moving through this life; they may be radically different from yours, which may bring them to radically different conclusions than the ones you've reached. You may agree with them, you may not, but at least consider that you might be wrong. Consider that you might be wrong about almost everything. Don't become complacent because complacency can quickly turn to the spiritually destructive apathy.

It may be tempting to turn your back on the world

at times. That's fine: take sabbaticals when you need them. But always come back. There are too many things worth fighting for to give yourself a permanent pass. When I started thinking about all of this, for example, I had to really force myself into an uncomfortable space. But I did it. Not because I wanted to, but because once I started questioning why boys are shooting up schools, it forced me to think about why boys and men are the way they are, which led me to question the way I am as a guy, which led to the inevitable realization that I have a son who might benefit from these inquiries, and other people's sons might benefit from the same. In exploring these questions for myself, I'm also trying to serve other people. Why? Because I, too, would like to be a useful engine.

ABOVE ALL, TO whom do I give my love?

The simple secret of manhood is love. It's almost embarrassing to write that down. Not because it sounds so hokey, but because, deep down, it's something all of us already knows. And yet . . . we men have an especially hard time admitting it to ourselves. For all of our bravado, for all of our sweat, our chest pounding, we still strive for that same, simple place. Just love. That moment of finding ourselves flailing in the world for the first time, breathing new air, and being held by our mothers and fathers. We begin our days seeking love and it pretty much stays the same. Everything we do and everything we are is in service of that love. But we forget. And so it becomes almost like a secret that each of us has to uncover on our own. The message of love is everywhere you care to look, as ubiquitous as commercials for air fresheners. Just quieter. And, no matter what anybody tells you, I think you have to uncover it for yourself. It's a secret I keep rediscovering. I learned it when I married Mom. When you were born. Three days later, when I made a right turn out of the hospital parking lot to bring you home, I learned it again. Rocking you in the middle of the night when you would not stop crying. When you first toddled to me on shaky legs. And then all of it all over again when your sister was born. On the first day of kindergarten when I put you on a school bus alone and trusted you would get home safe. A few years later, when both of you came home from school on a day when so many of our neighbors did not. It's a lesson I learn and relearn every day. I said that the machinery of the spirit lets inspiration in and breathes it out. Another word for that process is love.

There's a moment in *The Empire Strikes Back* when Darth Vader has captured Han Solo and is about to flash-freeze him like a trout. Right before his end, Princess Leia finally confesses the depth of her feelings for him:

"I love you," says Leia.

"I know," he replies.

It's one of the best lines in film history because it's so true to character. In his moment of greatest peril, Han's wrung-out heart doesn't allow him to return her love in full. Even in a galaxy far, far away, men are unable to express themselves. If I were Leia in that moment, I'd be glad they were freezing his self-absorbed ass.

"Be a man."

"Man up."

"Act like a man."

Traditional masculinity goes round and round expressing only itself: it's a language that contracts as it expands. The more it tries to define what it means to be a man, the fewer options it gives men for how to be. As it calcifies, it reduces everything to a binary—either something is masculine or it is not. The result is what we see, the retreat of some men into an ever-tighter shell. The Real Man's exploits and adventures are celebrated while his tenderness goes unremarked or mocked. It rewards a father working long hours in the city and taking graduate classes at night so that he can earn more money for his family, but it doesn't give him permission to tell his son he loves him.

Maybe love sounds corny to you. It's not. Or overly simplistic. It's not. If love were simple, it would be easy. Nothing could be further from the truth. Men ache for love but don't always know what to do with it when we have it. We ignore it, reject it, abuse it, malign it. And why should it be any other way? As men, we live in a paradox. Love demands an openness and vulnerability that traditional manhood opposes. How do we resolve this paradox of masculinity?

The answer doesn't lie in abandoning traditional masculinity, only that we broaden and deepen its language as we reorient our place as men. Manhood has always celebrated service to others. It has asked men to pick up rifles and plows and welding torches. We have done so because we understand that the work of men has been to provide and protect, and we have done our work. Now the nature of that work is changing.

Men are fumbling to find an alternative to our old ways, but we don't want to abandon everything we understand ourselves to be. We don't have to. We can preserve the best parts of our masculinity, jettison the stuff that's hurting us and the people around us, and work on developing the skills that *will* help us in school, in the workplace, and with our families. Empathy, compassion, understanding. Love.

Too many men think about love as a soft and passive force. It's not. Every parent knows the lengths they will go to for their child. We'll jump in front of bullets for our kids. Martin Luther King Jr. called love "the active outpouring of one's whole being into the being of another."

Does that sound like a soft and passive force?

Love isn't something that happens *to* us. It's something we *do*. Whether it's the love of a child, spouse, friend, community, or even an idea, love communicates itself as an action and a practice. Traditional masculinity teaches us to be strong and tough and brave. Think about how much strength love requires. How much perseverance. How much courage.

But also: how much empathy, vulnerability, grief.

Choosing love necessarily means choosing to expose yourself to pain. The two go hand in hand. So to help men love, we have to give ourselves the tools to deal with our pain.

As men, it's not enough to love. It's a lot, but it's not enough. Just as importantly, we also have to allow ourselves to be loved. For men, this might be the greater struggle. We have a far easier time lifting the heaviest burden we can find than accepting the love somebody gives to us when they offer to share the load.

Yes, men can go it alone. We can convince ourselves that we are "self-made men." We can be gunslingers, riding into town and riding out when the job is done.

But why would we ever want those things? Why would we ever turn our back on the one thing that makes life worth living? It's not enough to give love. You also have to open yourself to receive love in return.

I see that reluctance in you already. I worry about it, maybe because I recognize myself in the way you keep the world slightly at bay. When I was your age (and older) I treated nearly everything and everybody with ironic detachment. Somehow, that ironic detachment ended up giving me a career—I could be the funny, sardonic one. The one who could say the most outrageous things without cracking a smile. People seemed to like me when I said cutting things. Would people still like me if I opened up?

I was dating Mom at the time, and even as our relationship developed, I held some of myself in reserve. We both did. Even after we got engaged, I was still working on giving her my full love and accepting hers. That struggle didn't end on our wedding day. If anything, it got worse. Yes, we loved each other, but we struggled to understand each other, to hear each other, to be there for each other. A lot of that reluctance came from our personal histories. We fell back on old survival techniques to keep ourselves from getting hurt in our new lives.

That's why I say it took me until your birth for me to finally come to terms with what it meant to be a man. Not because I think fatherhood is a necessary component of manhood, but because, for me, fatherhood was the first time I had to learn to love another without condition or expectation. For me to be the kind of dad I wanted to be for you and your sister required a set of skills at odds with the sardonic persona that had served me well for so long. That guy didn't give a shit. This new guy did.

Also, babies are bad at getting sarcasm.

Somehow the soft skills of parenting—changing diapers, learning to swaddle you like a little burrito, giving you baths, rocking you back to sleep at three o'clock in the morning—those "feminine" nurturing skills wound up making me feel like more of a man than anything I'd ever done before. The work of parenting felt as much like man's work as spending the day chopping down trees. (Admittedly, I've never spent the day chopping down trees.) I didn't have to do traditional dad stuff to feel like a man. I just had to be your dad.

One great thing about having kids is they force you into an active practice of love whether you are ready for it or not. Among the best gifts children give to their parents is the gift of showing them their own worst self. When the two of you were babies, Mom and I could barely function from sleep deprivation and the mental fatigue of chasing around two chubby toddlers. At times, we yelled at each other. Sometimes we yelled at you. We took turns eating dinner because somebody always had to jiggle the baby while the other person wolfed down their meal. We saw the worst in each other and adapted. We learned how to be sleep-deprived and angry and impatient. We learned to get comfortable feeling inept, to navigate resentment, to persevere through moments of real disdain for each other. We sucked, but over time, the two of you taught us how to suck less.

The truth is, I sucked worse than Mom because I was less emotionally prepared for parenthood than Mom. Why was I less emotionally prepared? Because I had spent the thirty previous years in a cauterized emotional state. To get better, I had to figure out a way to become a new me. I had to figure out how to become a better man.

That process is slow and ongoing. It's an everyday practice, just like the practice of love is an everyday practice. The good news is I can practice them at the same time because they're the same thing.

You may be wondering how somebody gets into the practice of love. Believe me, I'm an amateur at this stuff, but I don't think love has to be mysterious. It's not something you find, like a penny on the street. It's right there, in front of you, but you have to be willing to let it in. How?

I've found that it helps to start with some of love's components and work on those: patience, kindness, empathy, resilience. All the stuff you already know. Maybe you just pick one of those things to work on in a given moment, or day. It's like anything else. You practice and practice. Sometimes it comes easy and sometimes it doesn't come at all.

Sometimes you fake it.

A lot of times you will fail in these everyday

practices. That's okay. Real men fail. There's no shame in failure. Most of the time, there's no shame in giving up, either. Part of the notion of masculinity is this "never quit" mentality. I disagree. There are going to be things you try, fail at, and decide are no longer worthwhile. No problem. I remember when you picked up the saxophone in sixth grade. You gave it a couple years but never loved it. Believe me, we didn't love it, either. So you quit. No biggie. Quitting stuff is fantastic. I feel like I've quit more things than I've started. Not this, though, because, in the end, this is the only stuff that matters.

Listen, I know how naive it sounds to say that "love" is going to fix men. Is love really going to help a guy graduate high school? Get a job? Is love going to feed his family? Is love going to drive the bad guys out of town instead of the gunslinger? Maybe not.

But maybe.

Not because love is magical thinking, but because it's the product of inspiration. All of us are at our best when we're operating from a place of spirit. When we persevere through difficulties, it's because we have a reason to do so. Mom, your sister, and you are my reasons.

You probably thought I was going to get through this whole letter without quoting Beyoncé. Wrong. A reporter for *Vogue* asked Beyoncé about her hopes for her baby son:

> "I want him to know that he can be strong and brave but that he can also be sensitive and kind. I want my son to have a high emotional IQ where he is free to be caring, truthful, and honest. It's everything a woman wants in a man, and yet we don't teach it to our boys."

That's all it is, man.

That caring, truthful, honest son with a high emotional IQ is only possible if we let our guard down sufficiently enough to allow that other side of our masculinity to fully emerge.

As you leave home, I'm asking you take a leap of faith: Who you are as a man is enough. It's more than enough. You don't need to get married or become a father to be a man. You don't need a high-paying job. You never have to question your manhood, defend it, or prove it. You only have to be who you are. All I ask is that you be *all* of who you are. The funny Elijah, the smart Elijah. But also the tender, caring, compassionate Elijah. Give yourself to others and let others give themselves to you.

There are so many ways to be a man, as many ways as there are to take a breath. Your masculinity is not a competition any more than your humanity is a competition, any more than one breath is better than another. They are all important, each leading to the next. Most of the time you will not even know you are breathing. So it should be with your humanity.

When I was a kid, somebody told me to "be a man," but he didn't tell me how. I'm telling you now. Be strong and resilient, yes. But also, be tender. Be kind. Be forgiving—of others, but equally importantly, of yourself. Breathe. Be inspired. Practice love.

SIXTEEN

◆◆◆◆

One Guy

Turn Around and Wave Goodbye

You leave for school in a few days. Mom bought new sheets for you, towels, a comforter, fan, reading lamp, a little area rug. Too much stuff, but she's not giving you stuff—she's giving you her love. Your school is too far away to drive back and forth and I don't know how we're going to get it all on the airplane. The bad news for Mom and me is that you won't be able to come home as much as we would like, but maybe that's good news for you.

I've been racing to get this done before you go. Something to give you as you walk out the door (along with that cash you requested). The truth is, though, you probably already had a sense of most of what I've put into these pages. We all do. As I said at the beginning, boys attain fluency in the language of masculinity around the time they gain fluency in their spoken language. We may not understand *why* we communicate the way we do, but most boys conform to the grammar of masculinity as readily as we do to that of our native tongue. You've been speaking "boy" as long as you've been speaking.

All languages evolve over time. Sometimes this happens on its own. Sometimes we have to consciously push them forward. Once, when you were about three, we drove past a cemetery. "Look," you said, pointing to it. "The dead yard."

There was another mass shooting yesterday, at a Walmart in El Paso, Texas. Twenty-two dead and twenty-six wounded. The shooter was a young white male. I was out of the house most of the day and texted with Mom about it. "This problem is going to get worse," I said to her, but I didn't think it would happen that day. Around midnight, *another* gunman—another young white male—opened fire outside a nightclub in Dayton, Ohio. Nine dead, twenty-seven wounded.

This morning over breakfast, I asked if you'd heard about the double shootings from yesterday. No. And you didn't seem very interested when I told you about them. "Is this going to be another morning where we talk about murder?" you asked.

"Probably," I said.

You sighed.

You've grown up with these massacres. Your attitude about them isn't indifference so much as resignation, the recognition that men are going to continue murdering strangers by the score. I'm not even going to bother adding the caveat "unless we do something about it," because I don't think we *are* going to do anything about it any time soon. Fortunately, my track record as a prognosticator is poor, so maybe—hopefully—I'm mistaken. In the meantime, a mass shooting inspired this letter to you and now, I guess, this letter is going to end in the shadow of two more.

These events linger with me now for days. I try not to watch the news coverage or the funerals or the speeches made by politicians on either side. There's no point in enraging myself any further, or allowing my sadness to carve out new crevasses to fill. Maybe it's hard for me to put these events aside because it once happened so close to home. Maybe because I've got a young white male of my own. Maybe because our paralyzed country allows it to happen time after time after time.

When I started writing this letter to you, after the Parkland shootings, I knew that it would be impossible to talk about boys without talking about everything else. I almost didn't even start because the task felt too daunting, too insurmountable for a former Teenage Mutant Ninja Turtle to take on. What possible use could I be to you on this topic when I can't even offer a better explanation of when to change your razor blade than, "You just kind of know."

But I also knew that nobody else was going to have this conversation with you because nobody ever had it with me. When I looked around, it seemed like nobody was having it with anybody.

I told you I wanted my dad to tell me the secrets of manhood. As a kid, I envisioned manhood as a series of activities you ticked off one at a time like Boy Scout merit badges. I just needed him to tell me what they were. I thought he could bring me into his hobby room, close the door, and lay it all out for me. "Not all men drive eighteen-wheelers," he might say, "but every man knows *how* to drive an eighteen-wheeler."

That's why it was startling to me when the term "man card" popped up in the culture. "Turn in your man card" became the cheeky sneer of choice against men who held their girlfriend's purse for them, or wept at McDonald's commercials, or ordered a chocolatini at the bar instead of a whiskey neat. The idea of manhood as a checklist of manly behaviors has survived because, in some ways, that's exactly what traditional masculinity is. The Infinite Axis of Manliness is alive and well and judging you accordingly. It's my hope that your generation can shatter it to pieces.

How do you do it? One guy at a time. One guy asking for help, opening his heart to another, standing up for others. One guy living a conscious life. One guy doing the simple, hard work of being a man. One guy practicing love.

You're going to mess up. Everybody does. I do constantly; I mean, you live with me so you already know that. That's okay. Messing up is part of the deal. But so is asking for forgiveness. So is accepting apologies from others, forgiving them for their mistakes. And so is forgiving yourself, which may be the hardest one of all.

I have no data to back this up, but I suspect so much of what poisons young men isn't the hate coming in, but the hate we have for ourselves going out. What stories do you tell yourself about yourself when you realize you cannot measure up to an impossible masculine ideal? We've seen so much work being done on this question with girls, and so little with boys.

¿Quién es más macho?

May we put that question forever to rest.

You're going to fall in love. Maybe a few times. Remember that love, all love, is a choice. It took me a long time to learn that love is an affirmation we make. Not once, but at all times. When you choose to love somebody, you are committing to give as much or more of yourself than you are expecting to receive in return. You are pouring yourself into another, as Dr. King said.

I hope you'll also embrace the good in traditional masculinity. Challenge yourself, test your limits, persevere. Have adventures. Do stupid, fun shit just because it's stupid and fun. Jump out of an airplane (and try not to throw up all over yourself like I did the one time I went skydiving). Use your body. Run. Eat too much ice cream once in a while. Once, I dropped acid with my buddies in the Badlands of South Dakota. Obviously, as your father, I could never in good conscience endorse your taking LSD, but I *am* saying it was one of the best nights of my life.

When I think about your leaving home, I have an image in my mind of you walking out the front door, your back to us. When I left home, though, all I remember is looking forward. I told you about the day my mom dropped me off at college in New York. She brought me up to my dorm room and I remember my impatience at wanting her to go. *Just go*, I thought. *Go, so I can begin my life*. What was she thinking about on her drive back to New Jersey? It never even occurred to me to wonder.

Every parent has a sense of wholeness at night when they shut off the lights and get into bed and they know that their family is together, and safe, and home. Once you leave, you'll carry that feeling with you out the door, and we'll never get it back.

Of course you'll come home, but it won't be the same again. Early school mornings out on the edge of the driveway waiting for the bus together. Packed lunches. Middle school dances. Our little family watching *Stranger Things* together, two episodes at a time. Driving lessons. Graduation. From now on, each time you come back, this home will feel less and less like your own. One day, you'll tell somebody you're going to your parents' house and you won't even notice you said it.

When we moved into this house several years ago, you were still more of a kid than a young adult, and you asked for a loft bed that you could climb into every night. We resisted at first because we thought it would be ugly and that you would outgrow it by the time you reached high school. You insisted, though, so we gave in and bought you one. The thing takes up half your room and it is, as predicted, an eyesore. We've joked with you that we're dismantling that monstrosity as soon as you walk out the door, but now that you're almost gone, I think maybe we'll keep it up for a while.

Neither of my parents survived into old age. When you are the child of parents who did not live very long, it's natural to wonder how many years you have before you join them in the dead yard.

I remember that last Christmas with my dad. His ridiculous teddy bear hat. That inscrutable Dad smile. None of us knows what tomorrow will bring. The kids at Sandy Hook and Parkland, the people in El Paso yesterday, and Dayton. We don't know so we do the best with what we've got right now. And right now, I have so much gratitude for you and your sister. My life as a man is better than it ever could have been without you. Kids teach us parents more than we can ever teach them. You've done that for me. Thanks for being my kid. Thank you for being my son.

I love you,

Dad

ACKNOWLEDGMENTS

I WENT INTO this project with some reluctance. Okay, fear. A few people prodded me forward, especially my editor, Betsy Gleick. It was her idea to turn my original op-ed into this book and her tough love that kept me moving forward when I was not sure I could. Thank you to her and everybody at Algonquin and Workman who have been so supportive from the beginning.

Before I began writing, I did a lot of reading. I've mentioned some of the authors in the book but I will mention them again here, as well as some others. For decades, many people have been asking the same questions about men that I only started asking in the last couple years. Thank you to Michael Kimmel, bell hooks, Barbara Ehrenreich, Dan Kindlon, Susan Faludi, Michael Thompson, Robert Webb, and Grayson Perry. I would encourage any readers who want to understand this subject in a deeper way to read any of these writers.

A few people have taken the time to talk with me about this subject. Thank you to Wade Davis, Kari Keone, Liz Plank, Ina Garten, Lauren Duca, Linda Balsama, and the many men I spoke with who shared their stories and affirmed my belief that men wish they had a better language and outlet to talk about this essential part of themselves.

Thank you to Barry Goldblatt.

Thank you to Ted Schachter, Rachel Salzman, and everybody at Schachter Entertainment.

Thank you, as always, to Martha, Ruthie, and Elijah.

I just wanted to add that I know this is a loaded topic and I suspect that there will be people who felt like I got certain things "wrong," or I didn't address specific issues. No doubt those people are correct from their perspective. My primary intention was to write a loving, inclusive book that serves as a primer for guys to begin thinking about basic questions about modern masculinity, the same questions that I've been asking myself as a man and the father of a young man. My questions may not be your questions, and my answers may not be your answers. I think that's okay. My secondary intention was simply to demonstrate that it's possible for regular, nonacademic men to have these conversations in ways that don't diminish their masculinity. Girls talk about girl stuff all the time. It's time guys started doing the same.